REAL ESTATE INVESTING FOR BEGINNERS

Quick-Start Guide

REAL ESTATE INVESTING
for BEGINNERS

ESSENTIALS TO START INVESTING WISELY

TYCHO
PRESS

Contents

Owning great landmarks such as the Empire State Building, or Trump Tower, or the General Motors Building, or the Plaza Hotel—there are certain just spectacular landmarks—it's an honor, it's really an honor. The Empire State Building is so special, it's now been surpassed in terms of height by a couple of other buildings, most of which nobody even knows what they are, and yet the Empire State Building remains the Empire State Building. It's just a magnificent building and really has become a symbol of New York. The Empire State Building, 40 Wall Street, there are a couple of them that are just really incredible buildings. Forty Wall Street is probably the most beautiful tower in New York. And having that and having brought it back to health, brought it back to prominence and health, it's something that I'm very proud of.

DONALD TRUMP INTERVIEWED BY PBS

Why We Love Real Estate

Real estate is an appealing investment in ways that stocks and bonds simply can't touch. To check your stocks, you have to review a brokerage statement or log onto a website. Real estate doesn't work that way. You can walk on it, into it, under it, or through it. People understand real estate because they can feel it.

Perhaps the material nature of real estate explains why it tends to hold its value so well. It's easy to forget about a stock or bond languishing in an online brokerage account. And even if you own shares of ExxonMobil, news of a huge discovery—or a massive explosion—in deep waters 10,000 miles away won't always move you. But real estate makes itself difficult to ignore.

How many times have you walked through a building and noticed its condition? Cracked walls and peeling paint tell a compelling story, even to investors without a background in carpentry or architecture. If such features leap out at the casual passerby, consider how much more you'd notice about a building you own. Every crack and blemish would demand your attention.

To assess the condition of a company that issues stock or bonds, you might follow news stories about the firm and then dig deeper. Once a conscientious investor commits her money, she will follow up with an investment of time and effort. But people who buy real estate, even amateurs, can assess the condition of the property without too much trouble.

Or at least that's what too many real estate investors believe.

The same tangibility of real estate that makes it so appealing can also fool investors into thinking they know more than they really do. Because while everyone can see that the linoleum in the kitchen has begun to crack and buckle, most people don't possess the expertise to determine the cause of the deterioration. Sometimes cracks in the tile simply reflect wear and tear, and replacing the flooring will restore the kitchen to its former glory. But sometimes the buckling stems from water damage or problems with the floor itself. Before you purchase property, you'd better know which problem you're buying.

Consider the preceding example a warning. You can't afford to buy real estate like you'd select a steak at the grocery store. On the surface, real estate doesn't appear complicated to analyze or purchase. But don't fool yourself. Location matters, as does an appealing price per square foot. But if you end the analysis at this point, a real estate investment could easily cost you money rather than make you money.

Fortunately, you don't have to navigate the tricky real estate market on your own. This book will walk you through the process of analyzing the market, evaluating rental property, and managing your real estate investments.

If the complexity of real estate doesn't deter you, then your investment properties can deliver excellent returns over the long haul.

During the 35-year period from 1978 through 2012, the National Council of Real Estate Investment Fiduciaries (NCREIF) Property Index averaged an annual total return of 9.4 percent. The NCREIF Property Index consists of more than 7,000 commercial properties; at the end of September 2013, it had a total value of more than $343 billion. This index may be the purest proxy available for investment real estate, which does not trade on public exchanges like stocks.

Those total returns—which include both cash flows and any appreciation in value—lag behind large-company stocks and long-term government bonds, which averaged annual returns of 12.6 percent and 10.1 percent, respectively, during the 35-year stretch. However, real estate truly distinguishes itself when volatility comes into play.

Volatility is a common measurement of risk. Standard deviation measures volatility by gauging how widely returns deviate from the average. The lower the standard deviation, the less returns tend to vary from the long-run average. And based on standard deviation, real estate is far less volatile (risky) than stocks.

The Property Index's returns averaged 9.4 percent with a standard deviation of 8 percent, which means that roughly two-thirds of the index's annual returns fell within 8 percent of the average, or in a range of 1.4 percent to 17.4 percent. By the same measure, two-thirds of annual stock returns fell between 29.3 percent and a *loss* of 4.1 percent, a range that leaves plenty of room for uncertainty.

While real estate's absolute returns trailed behind those of stocks and bonds, the difference between real estate and bonds wasn't great, and property enjoyed a big

REAL ESTATE DELIVERS BEST RISK-ADJUSTED RETURNS

RETURNS FROM 1978 THROUGH 2012

	Property Index	Large-Company Stocks	Long-Term Corporate Bonds
Average annual return	9.4%	12.6%	10.1%
Annual standard deviation	8.0%	16.7%	12.8%
Return per unit of risk	1.17	0.76	0.79

Sources: 2013 Ibbotson SBBI Classic Yearbook

edge in risk-adjusted returns. By dividing the average annual return by the standard deviation of returns, you can calculate return per unit of risk, a measure of risk-adjusted return. By this metric, the NCREIF Property Index rates 1.17 (9.4 percent divided by 8 percent) versus 0.76 for large-company stocks and 0.79 for long-term government bonds.

The very action of picking up this book suggests you feel the pull of real estate, the allure that has drawn in millions before you. Strong risk-adjusted returns are just part of the appeal.

In the third quarter of 2013, US households and nonprofit organizations owned $21.6 trillion in real estate, nearly one-fourth of their total assets. Against that property, owners have borrowed more than $9.5 trillion, equating to 44 percent of the total value of the real estate. Credit the Federal Reserve for those statistics.

While the wealth is authentic, real estate draws people for reasons other than its increase in value over time. And that, more than anything else, separates real estate from other investments.

Donald Trump, the tycoon who has survived four corporate bankruptcies, now controls a fortune that *Forbes* estimates at $3.5 billion. According to *The Real Deal,* about 90 percent of Trump's wealth is in real estate. But when he tried to explain his passion for property, Trump didn't delve into a discussion of profits or cash flows: "It's tangible, it's solid, it's beautiful. It's artistic, from my standpoint, and I just love real estate."

Artistry. That word explains the allure of real estate. And if you can make money with it, so much the better.

PART I

Becoming a Real Estate Investor

By pursuing perfection we set ourselves up for failure. This rings true for so many real estate investors because people are often really quite close. They're making income from their properties, they have some other way to make additional income, so there's just a tiny gap between where they are today and their dream of controlling their time as a full-time real estate investor, but they're scared to make that leap because it's not perfect yet.

I've got bad news for everyone. It is never going be the perfect time to take that leap. At some point you're going to have to muster up all that courage you can and go for it. Believe in yourself, and it's amazing what happens. And maybe it doesn't work out exactly like you think it's going to, but just by having the confidence and the belief in yourself to go for something you want, cool things could show up.

Of course you've got to figure out how you're going to pay your bills while you're there.... But if you wait until everything's perfect to do it, you're probably never, ever going to make the leap into full-time real estate.

JULIE BROAD
REAL ESTATE INVESTOR AND AUTHOR, WWW.REVNYOU.COM

1

WHY BUY REAL ESTATE?

Real estate investing isn't for everybody. It takes patience, discipline, and a willingness to maintain the property.

So does that mean that only the hardest-working, most diligent investors should buy a home? Of course not. Everyone who buys a home has technically invested in real estate, one of the few investments that delivers both economic value (housing) and financial value (price appreciation).

However, the level of effort needed to maintain a home—admittedly, it can be a burden—doesn't approach the responsibilities of managing rental property. Don't assume that because you bought a home in an appealing location for a good price that you're ready to pick out investment property. Don't assume that because you know how to patch holes in drywall and replace corroded light fixtures that you can handle maintenance for multiple properties. And don't assume that because you can meet a home mortgage payment, you're prepared to finance an office complex.

Size matters, and never more than in real estate. Consider the following scenarios:

- **Investor A** has $2,000. He'd like to buy a piece of a business, but nobody will sell an ownership interest for that little money. So he purchases 50 shares of Able Bakery, which trade at $40 per share. To make the buy, Investor A deposits $2,000 cash into a brokerage account, then purchases the stock on the open market the day his deposit hits the account.

  The investor's maintenance responsibilities begin and end with tracking the health and operations of Able Bakery. If the company falls on hard times, he can sell the shares immediately in the public market and invest in a different stock.

- **Investor B** has $20,000. She could buy stock, but the large chunk of money provides her with more options. Investor B's neighbor owns a steel fabrication plant that just won a lucrative government contract and could use some additional capital. With the $20,000, Investor B purchases a 1 percent ownership interest.

  Her maintenance responsibilities now involve keeping up with her neighbor's company. This will require more effort than Investor A's task because private companies generally keep more of their cards hidden. The size of Investor B's stake suggests she has the potential to make a lot more money than Investor A. But if business goes sour, she'll have trouble selling her stake because there is no public market for it.

- **Investor C** has $200,000. He wants an investment he can control, so he starts his own advertising agency. Investor C figures his seed money can cover the cost of office space, marketing, an artist, and a part-time secretary for about two years.

  His maintenance responsibilities are very high, as he runs the company himself and must keep an eye on everything. Of course, as the owner of the agency, his profit potential is also very high, as he can keep everything that's left after he covers the bills. But since he pays the costs himself, he absorbs most of the risk. He can't simply sell out if he decides the business has become untenable; the market for unprofitable businesses—particularly businesses where the owner does much of the work—is sluggish at best.

The one constant faced by these three investors is a limitation of scale. Investors can sometimes borrow against the value of a stock or an equity stake in a private business, but only a portion of the investment's value. Investor C might apply for a business loan, but even with a compelling action plan and cash-flow projections, he might need extensive outside assets to serve as collateral.

Against this backdrop, the appeal of real estate becomes apparent.

- **Investor D** has $20,000. Instead of purchasing stock or looking for a direct equity interest in a business, she sets her sights on real estate. Using her $20,000, she takes out a mortgage on an $80,000 piece of property. Such leverage increases the risk of an investment. But because real estate serves in part as its own collateral, investors can acquire an asset worth far more than their cash on hand, with commensurately higher cash-generating potential.

  This investor's maintenance responsibilities depend on several factors, including whether she intends to manage the property herself or hire someone else to do it (see chapter 8 for more on property managers).

Real estate can become as simple or as labor-intensive as you choose. Of course, the more work you do yourself, the less of your cash will flow to other people.

REASONS TO OWN

INVESTMENT

Home: Houses tend to appreciate in price over time, providing purchasers with a long-term benefit above and beyond the value of providing a place to live. Unlike rent, which benefits the owner of the real estate, every payment on the home builds up equity. Equity is the value of property above what you owe on it.

Investment Real Estate: Whether office, industrial, retail, or residential, such real estate provides the owner with a stream of cash income from rents or leases. Real estate investors can also benefit from price appreciation, but for most, the biggest appeal of rental property lies in the cash flow. In fact, rental real estate is valued relative to those cash flows. If the cash flows rise and the building remains in good condition, the building's value should rise. Rental real estate is a pure investment, not the housing/investment hybrid of a family home.

TAXES

Home: Homeowners may deduct from their income taxes both property taxes and the portion of their mortgage payment that covers the cost of interest. In addition, home-owners can earn a profit of up to $250,000 on the sale of a home without paying taxes on the capital gains (price appreciation). While the interest and property-tax deductions are nice perks, and real estate agents and lenders often tout them as key benefits of home ownership, the tax savings alone never justify the purchase of a home. As a rule of thumb, if the home purchase doesn't make sense without taking tax deductions into account, then don't buy the home.

Investment Real Estate: In most cases, the IRS treats income-generating real estate as a business asset, and investors can use most financing, operating, and maintenance expenses to offset their income. However, income property requires fairly complex tax treatment, and investors can count on spending some time preparing their returns or paying a professional to do the job. Owning real estate within a limited liability company (LLC) does offer some tax advantages.

LIFESTYLE

Home: Relative to apartments, homes tend to allow owners more independence and space. When you own property, you can usually redecorate or remodel or even add on, most of which won't fly with a landlord. In addition, homes tend to provide more space for the money than apartments.

Investment Real Estate: Investors buy and manage rental real estate to improve their lifestyle financially, generating cash and building wealth. They don't always succeed in this lifestyle enhancement, but the goal is simple enough. Of course, if you live in the residential property you own, then you can eat from both sides of the plate. In effect, you sacrifice the cash you could generate by renting out the space for the privilege of not paying to rent another place to live.

(continued)

REASONS TO OWN

(continued from previous page)

BORROWING

Home: Many homeowners borrow against their equity to raise cash. Such loans can make sense when the proceeds go toward paying down higher-interest debt. But every dollar you borrow against your home increases the risk that if your fortunes change, you'll lose that home.

Investment Real Estate: Like homes, income-generating real estate tends to appreciate in value if you take care of it, and over time you may build up substantial equity in the property. However, lenders may require more documentation and outside assets to lend money backed by equity in income property than they will for a traditional residential mortgage or home-equity loan.

Home and Away

You may have noticed that none of the preceding scenarios resembles a situation in which someone purchases a home. Yes, a home is an investment. But home ownership is to a rental property owner as what thumb wrestling is to Greco-Roman. Talk about stepping up in weight class.

When you purchase a home, you accomplish two goals. First, you provide a roof over your head. Second, you acquire an asset that will, if you take care of it, grow in value over time.

Home ownership makes sense for many people. But despite the investment component, it makes little sense to buy one solely for investment reasons.

The only real similarity between buying a home and buying rental property is the type of loan you'll take out—a mortgage. Mortgages are loans against property that use the real estate as collateral. Borrowers generally pay off these loans over long periods of time. Common terms for commercial mortgages from banks are 10 or 15 years, while many home loans come with a 30-year term. However, if you have good credit, lenders may give you a 30-year mortgage for commercial property—for a price.

Purchasing real estate for investment purposes is inherently more risky than buying a home, in part because your ability to cover the costs of maintaining the property often depends on the payment habits of third parties you can't control (renters). Of course, investment real estate provides the potential for impressive rewards as well.

Every investor must understand that risk and reward are connected. In most cases, the more risk you take, the higher your potential returns. And with real estate, you can play the game in different ways, ratcheting the risk up and down depending on your investment goals.

Rewarding Pursuits

People buy rental real estate for the same reason they make other types of investments: to enrich themselves.

Financial investments such as stocks and mutual funds are easier to buy and sell, and they don't require the level of capital needed to purchase real estate. However, you can invest in real estate for less money than you think. And while most investors should start out with mutual funds, stocks, or bonds, which fit neatly into tax-deferred accounts such as individual retirement arrangements (IRAs), real estate deserves serious consideration in your financial plans.

The potential benefits of real estate investing are myriad. The following list includes ten of those rewards.

Ten Rewards of Real Estate Investing

1. **Diversification.** In the investment world, *diversification* means the use of different types of investments to control risk. For instance, bonds often perform well during periods when stocks deliver weak returns, and vice versa. Strength in one investment can offset weakness in another. Real estate follows its own cycles and won't necessarily rise and fall with either stocks or bonds. As such, owners of stocks and bonds should consider real estate as a diversification tool. The layman would call such a strategy not putting all your eggs in one basket.

2. **Inflation protection.** While inflation tends to erode the value of financial investments such as stocks, real estate doesn't work that way. After all, what is inflation but a rise in the price of goods and services? While inflation saps the value of many investments and eats into consumers' purchasing power, the same forces that make canned peas and automobiles rise in price also drive up the value of real estate, as well as the rents tenants pay. Many investors like real estate because it helps them hedge against inflation.

3. **Higher cash returns.** By borrowing against the value of the property, investors can boost the purchasing power of their cash. For instance, if Manny has $50,000 to invest and the bank allows him to borrow at a loan-to-value ratio of 75 percent, he can acquire a property worth $200,000. Manny would put up 25 percent of the property's value ($50,000) and borrow the remaining 75 percent ($150,000). Not surprisingly, a $200,000 property can generate substantially higher cash flows than a $50,000 property. Suppose the property spins off cash flows of 8 percent, which equates to $16,000 per year. That $16,000 in cash flows equates to a 32 percent annual return on Manny's $50,000. Of course, Manny must also pay interest on the money he has borrowed.

4. **Monthly cash flows.** Rent payments provide investors with regular cash flow. Of course, tenants come and go, leaving a few offices or apartments vacant, and some

REAL ESTATE STEADIER THAN STOCKS

From the start of 2003 through the third quarter of 2013, the National Council of Real Estate Investment Fiduciaries (NCREIF) Property Index has delivered only six quarters with negative total returns. In contrast, the S&P 500 Index of large-company stocks posted 14 quarters with negative returns during the same period, declining about one-third of the time. Total returns reflect both income and price changes. The Property Index includes more than 7,000 investment properties.

Quarterly Total Return of NCREIF Property Index

	First Quarter	Second Quarter	Third Quarter	Fourth Quarter
2003	1.9%	2.1%	2.0%	2.8%
2004	2.6%	3.1%	3.4%	4.7%
2005	3.5%	5.3%	4.4%	5.4%
2006	3.6%	4.0%	3.5%	4.5%
2007	3.6%	4.6%	3.6%	3.2%
2008	1.6%	0.6%	–0.2%	–8.3%
2009	–7.3%	–5.2%	–3.3%	–2.1%
2010	0.8%	3.3%	3.9%	4.6%
2011	3.4%	3.9%	3.3%	3.0%
2012	2.6%	2.7%	2.3%	2.5%
2013	2.6%	2.9%	2.6%	

Source: National Council of Real Estate Investment Fiduciaries

Quarterly Total Return of S&P 500 Index

	First Quarter	Second Quarter	Third Quarter	Fourth Quarter
2003	–3.1%	15.4%	2.6%	12.2%
2004	1.7%	1.7%	–1.9%	9.2%
2005	–2.1%	1.4%	3.6%	2.1%
2006	4.2%	–1.4%	5.7%	6.7%
2007	0.6%	6.3%	2.0%	–3.3%
2008	–9.4%	–2.7%	–8.4%	–22.0%
2009	–11.0%	15.9%	15.6%	6.0%
2010	5.4%	–11.4%	11.3%	10.8%
2011	5.9%	0.1%	–13.9%	11.8%
2012	12.6%	–2.8%	6.3%	–0.4%
2013	10.6%	2.9%	5.2%	

Source: Standard & Poor's

may not pay their bills. In addition, expenses tend to be less steady than inflows. However, rental property delivers a somewhat predictable stream of cash, and any investment that pays you cash in most months has value.

5. **Less volatility.** The bursting of the housing bubble in 2008 and 2009 remains fresh in the minds of many investors, so the idea of real estate's low volatility might seem laughable these days. After all, according to the National Association of Realtors, the median home price in the United States fell to $164,600 in February 2010 from above $200,000 in mid-2008, an 18 percent decline. However, the S&P 500 Index, a collection of 500 of the largest U.S. stocks, lost more than 48 percent of its value in less than a year, from the high in May 2008 to the low in February 2009. Volatility is relative. And as the "Real Estate Steadier Than Stocks" table illustrates, real estate has historically delivered far steadier returns than stocks.

6. **Limited near-term taxes.** Every property is different, but many will provide tax-free cash flows. Don't misunderstand—real estate cash flows are indeed subject to U.S. taxes. But investors can deduct mortgage interest, depreciation, and other expenses, and those deductions may offset most or all the tax liability on the cash flows. Of course, when you sell, you'll face taxes on capital gains if the property has increased in value.

7. **Long-term income.** If you maintain your property, keeping it in good condition and upgrading or remodeling when necessary, it can generate income for decades, all the while increasing in value. Unlike most bonds and other fixed-income investments, real estate cash flows tend to rise over time. While rents ebb and flow in the short term based on market dynamics or supply-and-demand trends, over the long haul they have trended higher. According to the U.S. Census Bureau, median monthly gross rents have increased in each decade since the 1960s, rising 134 percent from 1950 through 2000. Keep in mind that the 134 percent rise (1.7 percent a year) is *after* inflation.

8. **Variety.** While investors tend to lump rental property into a single asset class, within that universe orbit planets with vastly different atmospheres. Prices and rents vary greatly from region to region, and you can pick your own approach. Some investors prefer low-price, low-rent properties, hoping to limit maintenance and renovation expenses, while others opt for high-end real estate in the hopes that its cash flows are less sensitive to the economy. If you'd rather not own the property outright, you can invest in real estate investment trusts (REITs), real estate businesses that trade on exchanges like stocks. Those who prefer to live dangerously can get into real estate investments that go beyond the typical cash-generating property—private real estate funds, fixer-uppers, land speculation, development, and so on.

9. **Permanence.** Land never goes away. Buildings don't last forever, but even if they wear out or burn down, you can remodel or rebuild. And if you own something that consistently generates cash and tends to rise in value, count on there being a market for it decades from now. Ten years in the future, mobile devices may become obsolete as people communicate in entirely virtual environments. Twenty years from now, clothing stores may disappear because everyone wears customized synthetic clothing created by cheap replication machines in the home. Thirty years from now, a *Star Trek*–inspired teleportation device may render all cars obsolete. But while home designs and technology may change and business practices may evolve in ways nobody can predict, the amount of land available will not increase. As Mark Twain said, "Buy land, they're not making it anymore." Fifty years from now, people will still need places to live, work, and congregate. The real estate business will change, but it won't disappear. And a clever investor with a quality piece of land can always find a way to charge people for using it.

10. **Intangibles.** For an investment you can literally feel and experience, real estate also has a surprisingly emotional appeal. People get passionate about their property, and passion breeds demand. Author and journalist Margaret Mitchell put it aptly in *Gone with the Wind*: "Land is the only thing in the world that amounts to anything, for 'tis the only thing in this world that lasts . . . 'Tis the only thing worth working for, worth fighting for—worth dying for." Nobody ever said that about a stock certificate.

Proponents of real estate investing can come up with plenty of arguments to tout it. You've just read 10 reasons to invest, and perhaps you could come up with more on your own. The appeal of real estate is undeniable, and by now you may be ready to jump into chapter 3 to learn how much you can afford to buy.

But before you take that leap, continue to the next chapter and check out 10 risks every investor should understand—because very few good things come without a price.

One of the greatest investments of our lifetime has been New York City real estate, and investors made the highest returns when they bought stuff during the 1970s and 1980s when people were getting mugged. The lesson is that you make the most money when you buy stuff that's out of consensus.

MARY MEEKER
INVESTMENT BANKER OFTEN CALLED QUEEN OF THE INTERNET, TAKEN FROM AN INTERVIEW WITH *NEWSWEEK* IN 2004

2

REASONS TO TREAD SOFTLY

Real estate offers excellent profit potential. But like any high-return investment, it requires you to take on substantial risk.

Chapter 1 provided plenty of reasons to buy real estate, some of which probably appealed to you more than others. But if you find a coin with a head on one side, you can count on the other side showing a tail.

Many of the risks that real estate investors face differ from those associated with more traditional investments. Here are some of those risks.

Ten Risks of Real Estate Investing

RISK 1 ▶ *Leverage: inflexibility*

Remember how leverage allowed Manny to parlay his $50,000 into a $200,000 property? Such borrowing can boost investment returns on a percentage basis, as the $16,000 per year in cash flows looks a lot better on a $50,000 investment than it does on a $200,000 investment. But digging deeper into the numbers reveals the darker side of leverage. Suppose Manny borrowed that $150,000 at 7 percent over 15 years. That loan would require a monthly payment of about $1,350, which equates to more than $16,000 per year—gobbling up all the real estate's cash flow.

Real estate investors must take the cost of borrowing into account whenever they analyze a piece of property. Manny can consider only real estate with cash flows comfortably higher than his borrowing costs. That requirement limits his options, and he

THE EFFECT OF BORROWING

An investor with $150,000 who can borrow at a 70 percent loan-to-value ratio may purchase a $500,000 piece of property. The following shows the returns that investor would earn based on changes in the property's cash flows.

Value of real estate	$500,000
Loan-to-value ratio	70%
Amount borrowed	$350,000
Amount paid from personal funds	$150,000
Interest rate	7%
Annual loan cost	$37,752

Property's annual cash flows after operating costs

Today (9% of property value)	$45,000
When economy picks up (12%)	$60,000
When economy slows down (6%)	$30,000

Annual cash flows after operating and borrowing costs

Today	$7,248
When economy picks up	$22,248
When economy slows down	–$7,752

Annual return on $150,000 investment

Today	4.8%
When economy picks up	14.8%
When economy slows down	–5.2%

Annual return if investor purchased $500,000 property for cash (no borrowing costs)

Today	9.0%
When economy picks up	12.0%
When economy slows down	6.0%

may pass over safer, stronger investments that simply don't generate enough cash to make a leveraged deal work.

RISK 2 ▶ *Leverage: downside risk*

Just as leverage magnifies gains, it can also magnify losses. Consider "The Effect of Borrowing" table, which illustrates what happens when a real estate investor borrows to fund the purchase of real estate. During good times, the use of leverage boosts returns as cash flows rise enough to more than offset borrowing costs. But when a property's cash flows decline—and rest assured, at some point they will, because conditions change over time—the borrowing costs typically stay the same.

Investors who borrow against real estate so they can purchase more expensive property must be prepared to accept greater losses when times get tough. As the table shows, an investor who purchases the property for cash may earn a smaller percentage return because he had to put up more of his own money. But because he doesn't have to make loan payments, he also faces a smaller chance of negative cash flows when an economic downturn causes vacancy rates to rise.

RISK 3 ▶ *Variable costs*

While rental income tends to be steady unless vacancy rates change, costs don't always cooperate. At some point you'll have to replace the roof on your six-flat building. Pipes freeze in the winter, lightning strikes city pumping stations and causes flooding, and trees fall, flattening garages. These costs will hit without warning and won't keep a schedule. Of course, a wise real estate investor will consider a property's cost history and its current condition so she can plan for contingencies. But no matter how carefully you plan, costs could exceed your expectations.

RISK 4 ▶ *Legal liability*

In many cases, courts hold the owner of the property responsible for bad things that happen, even if the owner had no power to stop them. Suppose your tenant leaves food on the stove too long and causes a fire. His renter's insurance covers his possessions, but not the damage to the building. Your own insurance should cover tenant-caused damage, but it might not recoup all the losses. And while most of the nuisance lawsuits that circulate on the Internet didn't really occur, not all are hoaxes.

According to LegalZoom, a bar owner victimized by several burglaries decided to set traps for anyone who tried to break in. A man under the influence of alcohol and drugs ignored (or failed to notice) the warning signs and set off a trap, which electrocuted him. The police didn't charge the bar owner with murder, but a jury eventually awarded money to the deceased man's family in a civil lawsuit. Of course, you're not going to be foolish enough to set deadly traps. But lawsuits happen. As a property owner, you must put some time into finding high-quality insurance, even if it costs more. However, even the best insurance policies have holes in their coverage and limits on what they will pay.

Chapter 9 will address corporations and limited liability companies, ownership structures that can help limit liability.

RISK 5 ▶ *Management issues*

Own property long enough, and you'll probably have to evict a tenant who refuses to pay. You may have heard horror stories about the difficulty of evicting someone, and many of them are true. Aside from evictions, you'll certainly face a series of unexpected hassles. If you manage the property yourself, be prepared for late-night phone calls, disputes between tenants about noise, and arguments over whether your failure to fix the air conditioning over the weekend justifies a renter withholding $500 from his monthly check.

And if you hire a property manager, be prepared for a thinner profit margin, because he won't take care of these problems for free. Unlike financial investments, real estate will often require a major commitment of your time, which has value. Too often, investors fail to consider the possible expenditure of time and effort that comes with a purchase of property.

RISK 6 ▶ *Financial complexity*

Owning real estate requires a lot more paperwork than owning stocks. Even if you're the type who prefers to manage his own money and prepare his own taxes, consider using an accountant to keep the books. In chapter 7, you'll learn how to prepare financial reports for property analysis, a task you should perform yourself. But leave the accounting and tax headaches to a professional.

RISK 7 ▶ *Magnitude of loss*

When you purchase a stock or a bond, even if the company that issued the security evaporates tomorrow, you'll never lose more than you invested. Not so with real estate. Because most people buy real estate using leverage, they gain control of assets worth more than the money they put in—in many cases assets that require a lot of cash to keep operating. This situation has ramifications beyond the legal liability mentioned in item 4 on this list.

Suppose you purchase an office building right before a neighborhood starts to decay. You can insure against burglaries and fires, but not against atrophy. If your tenants leave and you can't find new ones, you must still pay taxes and maintain that building, and the costs can add up quickly. You may be thinking, "If that happens, I'll just sell." However, most buyers aren't idiots, and they'll see the same problems you see.

Given the combination of borrowing costs and the need to pay to maintain property even when it isn't generating revenue, real estate investors potentially face losses far beyond their investment. Does this happen all the time? No. But before you buy real estate, you must understand this risk.

RISK 8 ▶ *Carrying costs*

You've probably heard the old proverb, "Never accept a gift that eats." Buildings eat plenty. Unlike financial investments, property incurs heavy carrying costs. Carrying costs reflect the price of holding inventory—storage of commodities, maintenance of buildings, and so on. For instance, if you own stocks, they just sit in your brokerage account. No matter how much you buy, the account can hold it without any additional expense on your part. But if you own gold, you must find a place to store it securely, which costs money.

Knowledgeable investors will go into the business understanding the principle that real estate requires a baseline of spending regardless of how you use the property. Of course, such factors are generally built into the price of real estate, and the discussion of cash flow in chapter 7 will explain how to take maintenance costs into account. But inexperienced investors who purchase property in hopes of generating a consistent, bond-like income stream may end up disappointed. Don't make that mistake.

RISK 9 ▶ *Economic sensitivity*

Most properties that generate rental income will see that income fluctuate based on economic or business conditions. Even if you keep your property immaculate and offer all the latest technology, companies without money to spend won't move into new space. Wise real estate investors take economic realities into account, considering whether they could afford to maintain the property during a downturn.

When you analyze a property and its cash flows, always consider what would happen if conditions worsened, then remained bad for a while. If you can handle such downturns, then the deal may make sense for you. Don't read this paragraph as a warning against buying real estate, or even an instruction not to do a deal with some downside risk. Just ensure that you know what you're buying before you sign anything.

RISK 10 ▶ *Perceived risk*

This risk is psychosomatic, but that doesn't make it less dangerous. People tend to anchor on the money they've already put in. Stock investors who purchased shares at $40 right before they fell often refuse to sell at a loss even if they could reinvest the money in something better. Such thinking leads to poor financial decisions, and real estate investors face similar threats. By now you understand that while you invest $50,000, you may actually control $200,000 in property, taking on the risks of a much larger investment. But understanding doesn't always equal action.

Suppose you find $10 on the ground at a casino. You might bet it all on a single hand of blackjack, hoping to double your money. But if you found $10,000, would you take the same action? Probably not, because you can do more with $10,000 than you can with $10, and you'd feel a lot more pain if you lost the larger amount. Real estate investors who use leverage to augment their purchasing power must be careful not to take small-money chances with a big-money investment.

Did the risks listed in this chapter make you nervous? If you're like most people, they did. And that's a good thing. Investors who don't understand or appreciate the risks of their actions often end up in a bad place.

By now you've reviewed the rewards as well as the reasons for caution. If the risks seem too much for you, realize that you can limit many of them by purchasing only what you can pay for without borrowing money. Plenty of people invest in real estate on a cash basis, earning solid returns on smaller properties than they could acquire using debt, all the while sleeping better at night.

Only you can determine whether real estate is right for you. In chapter 4, you'll learn to assess your risk tolerance. Consider not just the financial risks, but also whether the idea of real estate investing and the steps you must take to buy and manage property make sense for you personally.

If a review of the pros and cons of real estate has blunted your passion for property, then you've lost nothing but the time spent reading these chapters, and you may have gained a lifetime of peace of mind. But if you still feel a hunger to own rental real estate, then turn the page to figure out what you can afford.

Early in my career, I developed a firm grounding in business, with a special passion for real estate. Over time, I have studied architecture, planning, design, landscape architecture, and the elements that make the best cities work and be livable. And I have dug deeply into finance, art, politics and public policy, and the law. I learned discipline and leadership in the Marine Corps. All have helped me succeed.

Is a young boy, it seems I was always good at building things, everything from models and kits to fixing and rebuilding bikes and cars. I also had a fascination with architecture. Those interests led me toward homebuilding and community development after I served in the Marines. The process of building and seeing a finished product has always given me great satisfaction."

I do believe if we plan well and comprehensively, commit to the highest quality design, architecture and construction, don't be distracted by fads, and also commit to investment and renovation that keeps real estate fresh, we can enjoy our communities for ages. That's a lesson to be learned from the great cities of Europe that have survived for centuries and are so appealing.

DONALD BREN
CHAIRMAN OF IRVINE COMPANY, A REAL ESTATE TYCOON
WHO RATES NO. 69 ON THE *FORBES* BILLIONAIRES LIST

3

AFFORDING IT

Every salesman knows the credo "Don't accept a 'no' from someone not authorized to give you a 'yes.'"

The logic is simple. Only someone with access to the money—be it an individual considering the purchase of a washing machine or the CFO of a company mulling the acquisition of a competitor—can make a binding decision. And who knows? You might be able to sell the moneyman on your pitch, even if his underling would rather brush you off.

The same theory applies to investments. An investment broker or a real estate agent might insist you can afford this property. Less common, but not unheard of, would be hearing that you can't afford it, possibly because the broker or agent would prefer to steer the deal to someone else. But when it comes to what you can afford, take your cues from only one person. Yourself.

Sure, listen to what the other people involved in the deal have to say. Review the finances of any proposal and, if possible, talk to others who have made similar investments to find out why they bought in and whether they regret the move. But in the end, you must consider each possible investment on its own merits and decide whether it makes sense for you.

After all, it's your money.

Of course, asking yourself whether you can afford a particular real estate deal won't help much if you don't know the answer. And unfortunately, you probably don't. Not yet, at least.

You may already be using a personal budget and tracking your expenses down to the penny, which means you know how much you can afford to spend on a pizza, a refrigerator, or a car. But real estate finance—particularly the murky issue of rental property—doesn't flow neatly from a household budget.

Whether you can afford a real estate deal comes down to two factors:

- How much money you can invest.
- How much uncertainty your mind, heart, and wallet can handle, often called *risk tolerance.*

Only when you quantify both of these factors will you truly understand how much you can afford. The second factor generally makes more of a difference than the first, a fact that surprises many, though it shouldn't. If you can't handle risking all your money, then you can easily invest just a portion of it. And if your appetite for risk exceeds the resources in your wallet, you can augment your purchasing power with debt. (In case you missed the earlier warning, however, here it is again: Be very careful when you take on debt for a real estate purchase.)

Show Me the Money

To determine how much cash you should put at risk in a real estate deal, ask yourself the following questions.

QUESTION 1 ▶ *How much cash can I spare?*

Even if you borrow, most rental real estate requires a substantial up-front investment. Not everyone can afford it.

To illustrate the importance of this concept, consider two investors, Jenny Spend and Jack Save.

Jenny is a 60-year-old advertising executive at the peak of her career. She works 55-hour weeks, makes $120,000 a year, and has a $500,000 retirement account full of stock and bond mutual funds. Most of her salary pays for a big home mortgage and a fairly extravagant lifestyle partially funded via credit cards. Still, she's setting aside $2,000 per month for retirement and would like to diversify her assets. Jenny counts on her retirement portfolio to help fund her lifestyle after retirement and plans to start tapping into it after she stops working.

Jack, also 60, just retired after 35 years as a schoolteacher. His pension will pay him $40,000 per year, which can meet his modest living expenses but won't allow him to contribute to his retirement savings. He also has $500,000 in stocks and bonds saved up. Jack paid off his house a couple of years ago and carries no debt. To Jack, the investment account represents money for emergencies and hopefully something he can leave to his children.

Sally Sell, a real estate broker who knows both Jenny and Jack, just learned of a 12,000-square-foot medical office building up for sale. It's fully leased and in a nice neighborhood. The property generates cash flows of $7,000 per month, and the seller is asking for $500,000.

Both Jenny and Jack can borrow at 6 percent, with a loan-to-value ratio of 75 percent. These numbers imply that either investor could use $125,000 (one-fourth of their savings) as a down payment and take out a $375,000 mortgage with a payment of $3,164 per month.

Answer: Assuming the property's cash flows will cover both operating expenses and the mortgage payment, both Jack and Jenny can afford it. The deal would make rental real estate account for 25 percent of their retirement assets, which is above what many financial planners would recommend, but not dangerously high.

QUESTION 2 ▶ *How much more can I kick in if needed?*

Nobody likes to think about losing. But even the wisest, shrewdest investors, people who research opportunities exhaustively, get it wrong sometimes. The rest of the world gets it wrong much more often.

Don't approach your investments assuming failure, but do allow for the possibility that everything won't go according to plan.

To continue with our example, suppose Sally presents the deal to both Jack and Jenny, and the numbers look solid. On the surface, the property seems to have limited risk, given its 100 percent occupancy and generous cash flows. But nothing is guaranteed, and Sally insists that the potential investors consider what would happen if maintenance expenditures rose and an economic slowdown prevented them from raising rates when the leases expire in a couple of years.

Medical buildings tend to be less economically sensitive than other properties, but both Jack and Jenny are somewhat concerned about changes in the neighborhood that might make the property less desirable in the future. While the chance of such deterioration seems small, it shouldn't be ignored.

Jenny earns a nice living and expects to work for another 5 to 10 years, so she can more easily replace the cash flows provided by the rental property. And anyway, she'd planned to use the cash flows to pay down her credit card debt, and she doesn't really need the money as long as she keeps working.

However, her lifestyle already consumes most of her income, and she isn't sure she could adjust those spending habits if the property's cash flows went negative and she needed to pitch in to cover the costs.

Jack brings in just a third of what Jenny does, and he has few prospects for making more money. He had planned to reinvest the cash flows from the rental real estate to buy more stocks and bonds. The loss of the cash flow wouldn't affect Jack's long-term prospects, because he already lives on what his pension provides without tapping into his retirement assets.

On the surface, negative cash flows look like they'd present a problem, given Jack's low income. But since he doesn't need his retirement account to fund his living expenses, he could use the existing assets to make up the difference until the real estate became profitable again.

Answer: Both Jack and Jenny could comfortably absorb the loss of positive cash flows from the property. But in the unlikely event of a disaster, Jack has more flexibility to deal with the fallout, as Jenny can't afford to draw on her retirement assets.

QUESTION 3 ▶ *Can I cover the expenses?*

Sally has provided a detailed breakdown of the property's rental inflows and operating expenditures. The projected cash flow of $7,000 per month takes into account taxes, insurance, utilities, and maintenance costs. But the building will need some remodeling in the next couple of years. In addition, the former owner managed the property himself, performing some of the maintenance work, collecting rents, answering emergency calls, hiring contractors, and handling marketing when space became vacant.

Jenny's work schedule will not allow her to take a hands-on role with the rental property. Sally refers her to a property management company that will oversee the building's operations for $500 per month.

In contrast, newly retired Jack has time on his hands. He's no carpenter, but he can perform basic maintenance and repairs. If he mows the lawn, rakes the leaves, and shovels the snow himself, he can save the $400 per month the former owner shelled out for those services.

Answer: Jack's ability to manage the property himself—including taking on responsibilities the previous owner hired out—gives him both lower expenses initially and more control over those expenses going forward. On the other hand, Jenny's need for a property manager increases the costs of owning the property and shrinks her return on the investment.

In the preceding example, Jack can afford to purchase the property, and the deal looks good for him. Jenny can probably afford the property, but with far less margin for error than Jack. If Jenny's goal is to limit her portfolio risk through diversification, this particular real estate deal probably won't do the job.

Yes, the real estate could provide a counterweight to the stocks and bonds she already owns, but that addresses only one kind of risk. Purchasing the medical building would expose both potential buyers to the risk of loss, with Jenny feeling the pain sooner than Jack because of her higher expenses, and with Jenny less able to deal with the pain because of her need to live off the retirement assets.

FIVE DRIVERS OF THE BUY DECISION

Should you buy rental property or stick to traditional investments? The answer depends in part on your comfort level with the investments. But all five of the following factors can affect your decision. None of them on their own should persuade you either to buy or not to buy. However, if you take all five into account, you'll probably make better decisions.

1. **Wealth.** Simply put, the more money you have, the more you can afford to lose, and the easier it is to buy real estate. If you're sitting with $5 million in stocks, go ahead and put $500,000 into real estate. With that kind of money, you can buy outright rather than borrow if you prefer.

2. **Asset allocation.** There is no widely accepted rule of thumb regarding how much real estate an investor should hold. Many investors own no commercial property, while others plow most of their assets into real estate. For an individual seeking both solid returns and diversification benefits, holding 5 percent to 25 percent of one's portfolio in real estate makes sense, and 15 percent feels right for many investors. Any more than 25 percent, and you're no longer just an investor—you may have jumped into the real estate profession. Given the amount of money to be made in real estate, there's nothing wrong with that business—as long as you made the career move on purpose.

3. **Cash-flow needs.** Real estate isn't the perfect investment, but it does provide one benefit that appeals to investors seeking income: You can earn a higher cash return on real estate than on most stocks. Of course, if you don't need the cash to cover your living expenses, you can still purchase real estate and reinvest the cash flows in something else. But the more income you require from your portfolio, the more appealing real estate looks relative to other types of investments.

4. **Knowledge.** Every investment comes with its own learning curve. Real estate, however, is less forgiving of mistakes than most. Reasons for this include the following:

   - High purchase prices, which limit most investors to one or two properties at the most, offering them little insulation against problems at one of the sites.
   - Leverage, which amplifies the effect of any mistakes or bad luck.
   - Liquidity—or rather, the lack of liquidity. If a stock implodes, you can sell it on the open market and buy something else. But real estate can take weeks or months to sell when everything is going well, and the market tends to dry up quickly during tough times.

   The more you know about real estate and how the market works, the fewer mistakes you'll make.

(continued)

(continued from previous page)

5. **Time.** This factor applies in two ways. First, real estate is a better option for investors with a long time horizon. It tends to appreciate in price at a modest rate, which favors buyers looking to build wealth slowly and steadily. In addition, spending on renovations may come in chunks, and long-term investors are better positioned to profit despite that unevenness. If you replace a bunch of things this year, the next couple of years may require fewer expenditures. Second, property management requires a greater time commitment than many other investments will. The more time you can spare to manage your investment and the longer your time horizon, the more practical real estate investing becomes.

In the case of Jack and Jenny, the choice is clear: Jack should commit to doing more research on the deal, while Jenny should hold on to her money.

Admittedly, you are like neither Jack nor Jenny, and their examples can't provide you with a definitive answer as to what you can afford. But neither this book nor any other will provide a formula suitable for everyone, allowing for the input of age, income, and assets, and spitting out an amount to invest in real estate. The question of whether or not you can afford real estate requires a nuanced answer, and the issues Jack and Jenny face illustrate some of those nuances.

The "Five Drivers of the Buy Decision" box breaks down some factors that should nudge you in one way or another.

By now, you should have an idea of whether you can afford rental real estate. That puts you halfway to the goal. But even if you have $50 million in the bank and won't need a dime of it for 20 years, you shouldn't buy real estate if the investment would drive you to pull out your hair and gnaw off your fingernails.

No investment delivers returns big enough to justify sacrificing your peace of mind. Chapter 4 will help you find your limits.

From 1973 to 1981, the Midwest experienced an explosion in farm prices, caused by a widespread belief that runaway inflation was coming and fueled by the lending policies of small rural banks. Then the bubble burst, bringing price declines of 50% or more that devastated both leveraged farmers and their lenders. Five times as many Iowa and Nebraska banks failed in that bubble's aftermath as in our recent Great Recession.

In 1986, I purchased a 400-acre farm, located 50 miles north of Omaha, from the FDIC. It cost me $280,000, considerably less than what a failed bank had lent against the farm a few years earlier. I knew nothing about operating a farm. But I have a son who loves farming, and I learned from him both how many bushels of corn and soybeans the farm would produce and what the operating expenses would be. From these estimates, I calculated the normalized return from the farm to then be about 10%. I also thought it was likely that productivity would improve over time and that crop prices would move higher as well. Both expectations proved out.

I needed no unusual knowledge or intelligence to conclude that the investment had no downside and potentially had substantial upside. There would, of course, be the occasional bad crop, and prices would sometimes disappoint. But so what? There would be some unusually good years as well, and I would never be under any pressure to sell the property. Now, 28 years later, the farm has tripled its earnings and is worth five times or more what I paid. I still know nothing about farming and recently made just my second visit to the farm.

WARREN BUFFETT
EXCERPT FROM 2013 SHAREHOLDERS LETTER

4

CAN YOU HANDLE THE RISK?

Before you buy anything, be it a donut or a 500-room resort hotel, you'd better be sure you can deal with the repercussions. Admittedly, a few more grams of fat on the thighs may not seem like much of a consequence, but plenty of people have trouble deciding whether to eat a pastry. Those people should probably avoid investing in rental property; the decision making that comes with real estate ownership might incapacitate them.

Purchasing investment property could leave you carrying a lot more than extra pounds, so make sure you've considered whether you can handle the risk. Risk tolerance reflects your willingness and ability to absorb investment fluctuations.

As is the case with many financial concepts, there is no universal answer to the question "How much risk should I take on?" Your answer will apply only to you. Unfortunately, if you don't find that answer, you're likely to either take on too much risk and fall prey to knee-jerk reactions when times get tough, or take on too little risk and fail to meet your investment objectives.

Shrewd investors will consider their own risk tolerance before they make decisions. The next step on your journey to savvy investing involves asking yourself the following 10 questions. Answer these, and you'll have a good bead on how much risk you can handle.

QUESTION 1 ▶ *What's your chief investment objective?*

Investors' motives vary widely, and real estate makes more sense for some than for others. If you invest to build wealth over the long haul, real estate can be a good choice. This asset class provides fairly steady price appreciation along with regular cash flows, solid building blocks for investors in search of a strong financial future.

Some investors seek to diversify portfolios of stocks and bonds with assets that follow a different path, and real estate suits such investors well. In addition, those seeking to generate cash from their investment portfolios may also find real estate financially rewarding.

However, if you take a short-term view toward investing, avoid real estate. You've probably heard about people who "flip" real estate, buying it today, then selling it in a few weeks for a quick profit. That sounds good, but it works only under two circumstances:

1. You find property so badly mispriced that you can buy it for less than it's worth, then resell the property at a higher price. Of course, the same people you hope will pay more for the property also had the chance to buy it at the "bargain" price you paid, yet they didn't bite. That means either you're far smarter or luckier than all the other buyers or you misjudged the market. You can guess which of those reasons usually applies.

2. You have the expertise to purchase distressed property, which generally requires substantial repairs, and fix it up for resale at a higher price. This strategy works quite well for investors with the knowledge and resources to tackle the renovations quickly. If you can't accomplish that feat, you may end up flipping yourself, not the property.

Another problem that real estate poses for short-timers involves the marketplace. Real estate doesn't always sell promptly, particularly if you wish to receive top dollar.

Real estate investments work best for people who can cash in on both facets of its value—cash flows and price appreciation. And since the cash flows in a piece at a time and markets can remain weak for multiyear periods, long-term investors have an edge.

Bottom line: Investors with a short-term approach to investing will find real estate riskier than investors who take a longer view.

QUESTION 2 ▶ *How much do you know about real estate?*

This must sound like a trick question, given that you're reading a book about real estate investing. But a book—even a great book—won't make you an expert. This book will provide you with a framework for understanding how to invest in real estate, but much of what you need to succeed can be learned only through observation and experience.

If you intend to purchase rental property, be prepared to do the following:

- Follow market trends, keeping up with developments in the economy, rental and vacancy rates, and interest rates.
- Do additional reading and research whenever you run into a problem. Return to this book to refresh your memory, but some problems specific to your particular piece of real estate won't be addressed in these pages.
- Network with other people in the local real estate investment community. Sometimes you'll need to find a reliable service provider, and you can either call one you already know or seek a reference from another property owner. And sometimes you'll just benefit from the expertise and experience of others.
- Develop a list of people you can trust—real estate agents, contractors, companies that handle title work, property managers, accountants, and so on—to help you manage your properties and purchase new ones.

Bottom line: Real estate isn't a fire-and-forget investment. The more you know, the better your chance at success. Investors who lack the interest or discipline to truly become experts in the field will find real estate quite risky.

QUESTION 3 ▶ *Does market volatility keep you up at night?*

Worriers will have trouble with real estate investing. Remember the earlier warnings about how you can't expect to sell your property quickly, as you would with a stock or mutual fund? If your first impulse when times get tough is to sell out, don't buy property.

The prices of assets—real estate, stocks, bonds, and so on—rise and fall over time. Investors cannot avoid these short-term fluctuations. In most cases, if you own quality investments, you should simply ride out the gyrations and count on the market to correct itself in time. However, some investors can't exercise such patience and prefer to cut their losses rather than accept even a short-term decline in the value of their assets.

In most markets, investors desperate to sell fall prey to those who feel no need to rush into a transaction. With real estate, an illiquid market, that axiom goes double.

Bottom line: Your ability to live with market fluctuations is probably the most important component of risk tolerance. Never invest in anything that will cost you sleep.

QUESTION 4 ▶ *Do you consider yourself more of a saver or an investor?*

In real life, the concepts of savings and investing overlap. But for many people, the words saving and investing conjure up drastically different images.

Bottom line: If you classify yourself a saver—no matter how you define the term—you'll probably be comfortable taking on less risk and should either avoid rental real estate or stick to small deals.

FIVE WAYS TO LIMIT YOUR RISK

Like almost all investments, real estate carries risk. Investors who accept no risk will probably make no money. However, you can take steps to limit the danger of any inherently risky investment. If you plan to purchase rental real estate but wish to reduce your risk, consider the following strategies:

1. **Use less leverage.** If you have the resources, buy the property without borrowing any money. The lack of mortgage payments should allow you to keep more of the cash flow and leave you less susceptible to downturns in the market.

2. **Don't buy direct.** You can invest in real estate without purchasing the property itself. Start with real estate investment trusts (REITs), companies that trade on stock exchanges. REITs invest in real estate or mortgage loans and usually manage the properties they own. You can buy or sell REITs quickly like stocks, avoiding the liquidity risk of real property. And when you purchase a REIT, in effect you've hired an expert to select and manage properties for you. Chapter 9 will present more on REITs.

3. **Avoid low-rent districts.** Any time you purchase a property in poor repair or located in a bad neighborhood, you take on additional risk. Instead, target real estate in prime condition already leased to reputable businesses or people. The cash flows are easier to predict. Of course, you'll probably pay more for higher-end properties, but there's value in knowing what to expect from your investment.

4. **Spread your bets.** Rather than buy a single large property, consider purchasing more than one smaller building. Diversifying within the real estate asset class limits how much of a hit you'll take from a natural disaster or a change in the dynamics of a neighborhood.

5. **Use a property manager.** Every time you hire someone to do a job, you increase the number of mouths your investment property must feed. But a good property manager may spot problems earlier than you would and come up with better solutions. Hiring a property manager limits your profit potential but reduces both the investment's risk and the amount of time you must spend to manage it.

QUESTION 5 ▶ *Do you worry about not having enough cash to deal with emergencies?*

If so, you're not alone. Many investors fret about their ability to absorb financial setbacks without scaling back their lifestyle. But your thoughts on this topic will affect how you invest—as well they should.

Because of the cost of real estate, these investments can consume a large portion of the average person's savings. And while any investment property you purchase becomes a portion of the portfolio you can tap for retirement, it won't help you much if you need to raise money quickly.

Bottom line: The more you worry about having enough liquid investments set aside for emergencies, the less of those funds you should commit to a slow-to-sell asset like real estate.

QUESTION 6 ▶ *Will you need to spend a large amount of cash in the next five years?*

This one harks back to question 1, which addresses your investment philosophy. But even investors who think long-term may have real-life needs that trump their philosophical approach.

Suppose you have a child starting college or you owe a large sum of money that comes due in a couple of years. Because real estate is by nature a long-term investment, only a fool purchases property using funds he'll need soon.

Bottom line: The more cash you must have ready to pay out in the near term, the less risk you can handle, which means the less real estate you can buy.

QUESTION 7 ▶ *Can you live on your current income without drawing on your investments?*

This question might seem irrelevant because, after all, you're investing in real estate for the cash flow. But investors must remember that even properties that have historically paid generous cash flows may not do so every year.

It's one thing to invest in real estate to supplement your income. It's quite another to purchase real estate from which you'll need to draw a set amount of cash to fund your living expenses.

Real estate carries more risk than bonds or bond funds, which pay dependable cash flows that shouldn't vary much unless the company issuing a bond runs into financial trouble. In contrast, cash flows from real estate depend on how much of its square footage a building can rent out and on how much the owner must pay to maintain the property. If a couple of tenants leave and the roof starts to leak, cash flow may turn negative for a while.

Bottom line: People who rely on the cash flow from their investment portfolios to meet basic living expenses can afford to take on less risk than those for whom the cash flow is a bonus.

RIDING A MARKET DECLINE

Value of $10,000 invested in the NCREIF Property Index

2013	$227,668	1994	$41,616
2012	$210,324	1993	$39,118
2011	$190,265	1992	$38,585
2010	$166,516	1991	$40,303
2009	$147,218	1990	$42,688
2008	$177,067	1989	$41,728
2007	$189,296	1988	$38,720
2006	$163,416	1987	$35,321
2005	$140,164	1986	$32,703
2004	$116,742	1985	$30,196
2003	$101,972	1984	$27,146
2002	$93,565	1983	$23,846
2001	$87,653	1982	$21,079
2000	$81,705	1981	$19,262
1999	$72,793	1980	$16,517
1998	$65,365	1979	$13,987
1997	$56,231	1978	$11,611
1996	$49,366		$10,000
1995	$44,754		

Source: NCREIF.

QUESTION 8 ▶ *Do you expect your salary to grow faster than your living expenses in the coming years?*

This question, like most of its predecessors, speaks to risk tolerance for investments in general, not just real estate.

Suppose your salary covers your living expenses, with a little left over to invest. Be honest with yourself and consider both your job prospects and lifestyle goals. If you reasonably expect your income to rise at a greater rate than your costs, then you can accept more risk than someone who doesn't have much potential for income growth.

Bottom line: The less you'll need your investments in the years ahead, the more risk you can take growing those investments.

QUESTION 9 ▸ *Can you ride out a market decline?*

This question focuses less on your financial resources and more on your state of mind. While question 3 addressed your tolerance for short-term volatility, a true market decline takes the issue a few steps further. Remember the decline in real estate prices that contributed to the Great Recession? The NCREIF Property Index fell 24 percent in the 18-month period from mid-2008 through the end of 2009.

As the chart "Riding a Market Decline" shows, $10,000 invested in the NCREIF Property Index at the start of 1978 would have grown to $227,668 by the end of September 2013. This return assumes you reinvested all the cash flows back into the index.

Between the end of 2007 and the end of 2009, your investment would have lost $42,000 of its value. Of course, it would have regained that $42,000 plus a little bit more by the end of 2011.

The good thing about real estate—and most other investments—is that even if the value of your property declines, you need not absorb that loss if you hold on to the investment. Until you sell, the loss of value, while real enough, doesn't extend beyond paper.

However, a prolonged downturn could reduce your cash flows for several quarters, while at the same time making it more difficult to sell the property. Many investors would find such a situation scary, even if they possess the resources to wait until the atmosphere improves.

Bottom line: Sustained market declines don't occur often, but they do happen. If you have the patience and fortitude to hunker down and manage the property as best you can until things get better, you can handle more risk than someone who will lose faith if the market takes a year or more to improve.

QUESTION 10 ▸ *Do you consider yourself a risk-taker?*

At first, this question sounds self-fulfilling. But over time, perception tends to become reality. If you consider yourself a risk-taker, you probably either already take risks or will do so more often in the future.

Bottom line: Within reason, your ability to accept risk hinges on your willingness to take that risk. Of course, if you continue to wager double or nothing every time a bet presents itself, at some point you'll end up with nothing more to risk. That's why you need to ask yourself all 10 questions to provide perspective on your true appetite for risk.

After answering the 10 questions, you should have a pretty good idea of your risk tolerance. Since you can't simply plug the answers into a spreadsheet and churn out a report that says you have a risk tolerance greater than that of 87.4 percent of investors, the next step requires some honesty and flexibility on your part.

This book can't tell you whether to invest or even how to invest. It just gives you the tools to use, as well as some instructions regarding their use. Consider the Q&As in this chapter and chapter 3 as tools to assess your preparedness for real estate investing.

Before you turn to the next chapter, use the information you gleaned from your answers to the questions and do two things.

First, determine how much you think you should invest in real estate. Don't feel you must limit yourself to a single number. A range is okay, as long as it remains within 5 percent to 25 percent of your total investable assets.

Second, determine whether your risk tolerance is high, average, or low. In part 2 of this book, you'll learn how to find, analyze, and purchase property. Some types of property and some investment strategies entail more risk than others. Armed with a comprehensive, honest assessment of your risk tolerance, you can determine which types of property make the most sense for you.

PART II

Analyzing and Acquiring Property

No bodybuilder will tell you that being in the gym 5-6 days a week is exciting. It's not that we don't enjoy the results. It's that the real work wasn't exhilarating. In fact, if you were serious, it often felt like flirting with death. Same with running. Are you a runner? Done a few marathons?

Were ya just thrilled to the bone upon awakening Sunday mornings so you could get that 20-mile training run in? No, most of the time you weren't. But you loved the feeling of being in better shape, and were indeed thrilled by how you felt as you crossed the marathon finish line. Having competed in both sports, I can look you straight in the eye and tell you how boring so many of the weight workouts and long training runs were.

But, like bodybuilding and running, real estate ... isn't about having loads of fun on the way. It's about results. Even though gettin' there was many times so boring your IQ dropped, the results were well worth the years of effort. The short cuts so many of us use to create wealth and robust retirement income, are in actuality fantasies missing the happy ending.

JEFF "BAWLDGUY" BROWN
REAL ESTATE INVESTOR AND BROKER/OWNER OF WWW.BAWLDGUY.COM

5

LOTS OF OPTIONS

So far, this book has presented investment real estate as a single entity, an asset class of its own, separate from stocks or bonds. And compared to stocks and bonds, all investment real estate should be grouped together.

But now that you know something about real estate, now that you've learned a number of ways in which rental real estate differs from financial assets, it's time to dig a little deeper.

Not all real estate investments will behave the same way. Of course, every piece of rental property shares a few of the same characteristics:

- It can generate returns in two ways—cash flows and capital gains. Appreciation in value depends on making cash flows rise. You stand a better chance of boosting cash flows if you keep up with maintenance and the neighborhood (retail and multifamily) or region (office, industrial, retail, and multifamily) remains vibrant.
- It requires active management, either by the owner or her designated agent, to remain healthy and profitable.
- It serves as a hedge against inflation.
- It will cause you headaches if you buy for the wrong reason or before you are ready for the responsibility.

However, beyond those characteristics, the various types of real estate may require different approaches. More to the point, different types of property will appeal to investors in different ways.

You don't have to look very far to find some pundit saying that office property is the place to be while investors should avoid retail real estate. And right next to that guy, someone else is saying the opposite. Before you try to identify which section of the market will outperform, take into account these three facts:

1. From 1994 through 2009, the five traditional types of rental property in the NCREIF Property Index all delivered annualized returns between 12.1 and 13.1 percent. Plenty of people will try to predict the future, but it's difficult to believe anyone who says one type of property will leave the others behind over the long haul.

2. For short to moderate periods of time, and possibly over the course of several years, one property type will lead, while others lag. But even professional investors who spend much of their time and money analyzing market forces have mixed success at identifying which sector will outperform. As an individual investor, don't waste time playing that game.

   Each piece of property is different, even from another one across the street that looks almost the same. Use the strategies presented in chapters 6 and 7 to assess each investment's potential, then buy the ones that make the most sense to you. If you have the time, resources, and inclination to make multiple investments, consider purchasing different types of real estate to limit your exposure to trends that cause one group to perform poorly.

3. No matter how much effort you put into your analysis, at some point your property will run into trouble and deliver subpar returns. Don't bail out just because the investment isn't doing what you expected. Whenever you encounter a rough patch, repeat the steps you took when assessing the investment in the first place.

If you see a fundamental shift—long-term demographic changes to the region or neighborhood that will affect demand permanently, structural problems with the building that will require substantial expense to fix, issues with financing, and so on— then give serious thought to an exit strategy. Barring such a long-term danger, you're probably better off riding out the storm. Of course, if you keep up with your property and local and national real estate trends, you'll probably have some warning about these debilitating issues before they fully manifest.

Still game for real estate investing? Then it's time to learn about the different types of property.

The Big Five

Most investors should, at least at first, stick to four of the five traditional types of rental real estate.

In the world of office real estate, the class structure is alive and well. Most office space can be segmented into Class A, Class B, or Class C. There is no universal standard for what separates one class from another, and plenty of buildings that seem more suited to a lower class will try to pass themselves off as belonging to a higher-rated group in an effort to attract better tenants and charge higher rents. The following are some general characteristics to help you ascertain the quality of an office building you're considering for purchase.

	Class A	Class B	Class C
Rent	Top 10% of rents	Rents in 60% to 90% range	Below-average rents
Tenants	Tenants with top credentials	Good to average tenants	Local businesses, tenants without good credit
Condition	Perfect	Well maintained	Needs work
Amenities	All the latest technology	Some amenities	Limited

Source: Professor James R. DeLisle, University of Missouri–Kansas City

Office

This sector grabs the spotlight and continues to dominate the headlines. Office property accounted for 37 percent of the value of the NCREIF Property Index in 2010, by far the largest sector.

If you read about a real estate deal on a section front in the *Wall Street Journal* or hear a real estate story as the lead item on a national business program on the radio or TV, the news probably involves an office project. The sheer size and expense of many office projects makes the sector stand out from the crowd.

Investors seeking to purchase office buildings need not limit their sights to downtown. The NCREIF says suburban properties make up 60 percent of the total market value of office real estate and 85 percent of the actual buildings.

On average, office buildings are worth more than other properties, making many of them out of range for all but the wealthiest investors. If you don't have seven figures to spend, you'll probably have better luck concentrating on suburban markets, where you can find a greater selection of properties small enough to afford.

Office space falls into three categories: Class A, Class B, and Class C. The "Best in Class" table illustrates some of the differences among these classes. Unfortunately, the typical individual investor will find Class A and most Class B buildings out of his price range. Fortunately, you can still make money with Class C property. Remember, the key isn't how much rent you charge but how much cash you slip into your wallet after you pay all the bills.

PROS

- **Sex appeal.** Just like clothes can make the man, the façade can make the building. Office complexes tend to be tall and shiny, all glass and steel, designed to draw the eye of everyone driving past. Office real estate investors, probably because of their high-visibility projects, can keep the highest profiles. If you don't care about notoriety, this may not sound like a perk.
- **Growth potential.** Many of the faster-growing industries—technology, professional services, finance, and management—tend to be heavy users of office space. For decades the U.S. economy has been transitioning from producing goods to providing services, a long-running trend that should continue to drive demand for office space.

CONS

- **High prices.** In 2010, the average office building in the NCREIF Property Index was worth more than $58 million. Not surprisingly, individual investors often have trouble buying office buildings.
- **Volatility.** From 1994 through 2009, office properties in the Property Index delivered returns similar to those of other traditional property types but saw the second-most volatility. Only hotels saw a wider dispersion of returns.

CHARACTERISTICS

- Suburban properties tend to deliver lower returns than buildings in central business districts. Of course, the price of buildings in big-city downtowns may make it difficult for you to take advantage of this trend.
- Location matters for office space, but mostly in a general sense. Regions with a high quality of life, educated workforce, and growing population tend to attract companies that need office space. Office renters may care more about the characteristics of the city or the neighborhood than the benefits of one lot versus another a half mile away.

Retail

Shopping centers and other retail property made up about 20 percent of the NCREIF Property Index in 2010. This type of real estate will appeal to investors with an understanding of consumer trends.

More so than any of the other traditional property types besides hospitality, the success of retail investments depends on the name over the door. Have you ever seen a store located in what looks like a prime spot but suffers from empty parking lots day in and day out? Most people have probably witnessed that phenomenon more than once.

Office and industrial buildings tend to be located in places within comfortable commuting range for employees, and sometimes customers or suppliers. In general, people travel to office or industrial buildings because they have jobs or appointments there, not because they happened to be driving past and liked the look of the property. But retailers take a more street-level approach, because for businesses that rely on consumer traffic, this corner might mean success while that corner might lead only to bankruptcy.

When an upscale grocery store locates in a low-income neighborhood, it may fare poorly because the competitor down the road sells its canned peas for $0.10 less. Then when the high-priced retailer leaves, a rival that knows how to service customers of modest means may move into the space and make a nice profit. You rarely hear such stories with office or industrial property.

Retail outlets come in many flavors, which explains why they can thrive in just about any location. However, the very variety that allows retailers to sprout up on every corner puts a premium on their ability to gauge the market and select a location.

Do you need to become a retailing expert to make money with retail space? No. But you'd better understand the business well enough to know a dud when you see one. Pay attention to both local economic trends and the demographics of your community. That knowledge will give you an edge in attracting tenants and spotting potential problems.

A failing store is more likely to skip a rent payment than a successful one. And even if you end up collecting all your cash flows, you're better off if you can attract successful tenants who will stay in your building for multiple years. Long-term renters provide steady cash flow and reduce the time and money you spend trying to attract new tenants.

PROS

- **Close to home.** You can find shopping centers and strip malls pretty much everywhere. Want to invest in your own community? There's a good chance someone has a retail building for sale.
- **Variety.** More so than with office or industrial space, you can find small properties that don't require a huge up-front investment.

CONS

- **Consumer sensitivity.** Owners of retail property need to understand more than just the real estate business. Tenant selection matters in all types of real estate investing, but never more than with retail properties.

- **Economic sensitivity.** Because so many retailers live or die based on whether consumers choose to buy products they don't really need, your tenants' fortunes can change overnight.
- **Turnaround.** Because both economic and demographic trends change, even a well-run, healthy retail center may not maintain the same group of tenants for too long. Competitors will set up shop nearby or a style of clothing will give way to a new trend, and suddenly one of your renters will shut down or relocate. Investors must be prepared for this type of turnaround.

CHARACTERISTICS

- Large malls comprise nearly half of the value of retail real estate in the NCREIF Property Index but only about 10 percent of the properties. The vast majority of properties are smaller and cheaper.
- In recent years, many office and residential buildings have gone to a mixed-use format, with retail on the ground floor and a different type of tenant (typically office or residential) on the upper floors. However, most of these buildings are too large and expensive for beginning real estate investors.
- Grocery stores and dollar stores tend to be less sensitive to economic conditions than most other retailers. After all, while cash-strapped customers may cut back on new clothes, they still must purchase food. And when money gets tight, many consumers will trade down, seeking bargains on items they used to purchase at higher-end retailers.

Industrial

While industrial buildings account for 19 percent of the Property Index's value, your typical individual investor doesn't think about them very often.

The word industrial conjures up images of manufacturers with plants belching smoke into the air. But as a real estate investor, you probably won't be looking at any factories, as most are occupied by the companies that own them. When it comes to rental real estate, *industrial* generally refers to warehouses or distribution centers. As of 2010, warehouses accounted for 80 percent of the value of industrial properties in the NCREIF Property Index.

Compared to the average retail or office property, industrial buildings tend to be smaller; many house just one tenant. These characteristics provide opportunities for real estate investors who don't care whether their investments keep a high profile.

Zoning codes keep many industrial buildings isolated from other properties, in part because they tend to be noisy and produce more pollution than other enterprises. You'll find most industrial buildings in industrial districts of cities and in industrial parks. These industrial parks have sprouted up all over the country, allowing many investors to purchase their industrial property locally.

In addition, plenty of warehouses or distribution centers locate in stand-alone buildings outside of industrial areas.

PROS

- **Affordability.** On average, industrial properties cost about a third of the average office building. This lower price stems from both the average property's smaller size and the fact that in most markets, industrial buildings sell for less per square foot than office or retail.
- **Availability.** You can find industrial buildings everywhere, even in areas not known for their industry. They don't rely on customer traffic, and many industrial buildings nestle quietly among more flamboyant properties or sit alone in fields, often with understated signs or no identifying marks at all.
- **Growing importance.** In the global economy, logistics has taken on new importance. Customers expect companies to ship to more remote areas than ever before but won't accept long waits for delivery. More and more companies are setting up their own storage and distribution centers to keep goods closer to their customers. Some of the larger firms buy or build their own buildings, but plenty of smaller companies will need to rent industrial space.

CONS

- **Crime.** More than other types of rental property, industrial buildings often cluster in questionable areas. The combination of deteriorating industrial districts, less foot and car traffic, and locations separated from other properties can encourage criminal activity. If you wish to purchase industrial property, consider your location carefully. If needed, invest in either a security system or live guards. While security can become an issue for any kind of investment property, it's more likely to pose a problem in industrial areas, particularly with warehouses that store valuable goods.
- **Economic sensitivity.** Demand for industrial property stems from the need for storage and transportation of goods. When business activity slows, industrial tenants may find themselves strapped for cash and in need of less space.

CHARACTERISTICS

- Many industrial buildings house more than just traditional warehouse or distribution operations. Mixed-use buildings include office complexes with loading, storage, or mailroom facilities. However, as is the case with mixed-use retail, these buildings tend to be expensive, out of the reach of most individual investors.
- Most industrial buildings are located near major transportation routes. If you live in an area with a railroad terminal or container port, expect to find a higher concentration of industrial buildings than in other parts of the country.

- There's a reason why industrial property sells for less than office or residential space: You can't charge as much rent. For example, as of November 17, 2013, the average office property in Illinois rented for $16 per square foot per year, with retail space at just over $15 per square foot. In contrast, industrial space cost less than $7 per square foot. (Source: LoopNet.com)

Multifamily

Apartment complexes, which account for nearly 20 percent of the value of the NCREIF Property Index, have particular appeal with individual investors, for one obvious reason.

Everyone understands residential real estate, at least the basics. Why? Because we've all lived in an apartment or a house, and we know what people expect from their residences. Unfortunately, having a grasp of when to fix the leak yourself versus when to call in a plumber doesn't make you a good manager of multifamily property.

Some owners of multifamily property live on-site and deal with tenant issues personally, while those with handyman skills can do some of the repairs themselves. But such a strategy makes sense only if you can commit a large portion of your time to the property. Most individuals who purchase residential rental property should hire a property manager. Some complexes provide free or discounted housing to a superintendent who, in exchange, will tackle building repairs and maintenance, tenant relations, and/or leasing.

One long-term trend suggests demand for multifamily property has staying power. Younger Americans have become comfortable with apartment living and feel less pressure to buy homes. This demographic shift has sparked a couple of trends that favor owners of apartment complexes.

According to the U.S. Census Bureau, 65.3 percent of households owned homes in the third quarter of 2013, well below the rate of more than 69 percent in 2005. Home ownership has been trending lower over the last eight years, reverting to levels common in the mid-1990s, before the drive to put more people in single-family homes picked up speed. Low interest rates, government initiatives, and aggressive lending by banks made it easier and more attractive to own a home—until the market meltdown in 2008.

The apartment vacancy rate fell below 8.5 percent in the second and third quarters of 2013, the lowest in more than eight years. Rents have been rising steadily for more than a decade, and a combination of high rents and low vacancy implies a strong market.

Going forward, could home ownership rates rise as more households forgo apartments in favor of owning their own house? Of course. But the current mark near 65 percent isn't unduly low by historical standards, and only time will reveal the country's equilibrium home ownership rate.

PROS

- **Steady demand.** Of all the traditional property types, multifamily is least susceptible to economic downturns. People will always need somewhere to live.
- **Familiarity.** Since you've lived in either a house or an apartment, you'll possess at least a basic understanding of what tenants will need.
- **Safety in numbers.** When you have five office tenants and one refuses to pay rent or doesn't renew the lease, you'll feel the loss of cash flow until you resolve the situation. When you have 50 apartments and one tenant moves out or won't pay, the decline in cash flow shouldn't hurt as much. In addition, when you deal with a large number of tenants, at any given time you'll probably have people moving in and out, a level of activity that should keep vacancy rates steadier than with other types of property.

CONS

- **Tenant problems, part one: round-the-clock responsibility.** Because they inhabit the property at all times of the day or night, apartment dwellers can find a lot of reasons to call the property owner or manager to complain or request services. Of course, industrial and office tenants will also expect landlords to address problems quickly. But an accounting office rarely calls at 3 a.m. on a Sunday complaining that the heat has been cut off and demanding that you fix it immediately.
- **Tenant problems, part two: volume.** Most businesses use chunks of office, industrial, or retail space larger than the typical apartment. While an office building with 50,000 square feet of rentable space might have 10 tenants, a multifamily property of the same size could have 50. More tenants means more phone calls and more apartment-specific issues. In addition, the larger your number of tenants, the more likely you are to encounter the truly horrid tenant who costs you thousands of dollars and ties you up in court.
- **Short-term commitments.** While office, industrial, and retail tenants routinely sign multiyear leases, residential tenants don't plan that far ahead. One-year leases are the norm, with many properties allowing shorter-term deals or even month-to-month renting. Long-term leases provide stability and peace of mind, and you just won't get that with residential property.

CHARACTERISTICS

- All real-estate ownership exposes the investor to legal liability. But multifamily brings an extra layer of exposure, as many states and municipalities have their own ordinances that govern the rights of tenants. Be aware of the laws in your area.
- Multifamily investors may encounter the domino effect with water disasters, getting multiple tenants angry at the same time. A third-floor tenant's overflowing bathtub can cause damage next door, as well as on lower floors. Office, retail, and

warehouse properties shouldn't see the same type of water usage, and the size of the individual units reduce the likelihood of damage affecting more than one tenant.

Hotel

By far the smallest of the five traditional property sectors, hospitality accounts for about 3 percent of the value of the NCREIF Property Index. Of the five traditional types of property, individual investors will have the toughest time buying hotels.

The sector's small size relative to the others results in far fewer properties becoming available. High prices also keep investors at bay. According to the American Hotel and Lodging Association (AHLA), in 2012 the average hotel had 93 rooms. That average excludes tiny properties with fewer than 15 rooms. While a relatively small number of huge properties skew the average higher, most hotels in urban areas are too large for the typical individual real estate investor to buy.

Of course, you can find thousands of small hotels in suburban, exurban, and remote areas. However, the success of hotels depends in large part on the health and demographics of their region. On average, hotels saw occupancy rates of 61 percent in 2012. An efficiently run hotel that routinely fills up most of its rooms can make very good money. But hospitality has high fixed costs, and the key to success is volume. In other words, you can serve 50 guests for only a moderately higher cost than you can serve 25.

Have you ever traveled to a hotel in a small town and seen just two cars in the parking lot? It happens all the time. Given an average occupancy rate of 61 percent, thousands of hotels keep fewer than half of their rooms full most of the time. Not surprisingly, if you want one of the hotels with a high occupancy rate, you'll have to pay a lot more for it.

PROS

- **Strong industry fundamentals.** In 2012, the lodging industry earned profits of $39 billion, up 14 percent from 2011, while revenue rose 5 percent, according to the AHLA. Credit both higher occupancy and an increase in per-room rates for the gains.
- **Static supply.** As of late 2013, developers weren't building many hotels. Of course, that could change at any time.

CONS

- **Lack of availability.** A relatively small number of properties for sale, coupled with the large size of the average property, means individual investors seeking a profitable hotel don't have a lot of choices.

- **Management responsibilities.** Hotels don't usually operate like office or industrial buildings, leasing space to tenants who operate their own businesses. If you buy a hotel, you'd better be prepared to manage it, down to booking guests, staffing the lobby, and making sure the rooms remain clean. Yes, you can hire the job out, but not as simply as you might call a property management company for your apartment complex. Investing in a hotel is less about real estate than about the hospitality business. Not everyone is up for that.

CHARACTERISTICS

- Investors seeking to enter the hotel business might be better off buying a franchise. Some national chains license franchisees to operate hotels under their brand.
- Beware hotels with restaurants on the premises. Restaurants are notoriously difficult to operate profitably, and many a hotel has failed because an eatery gobbled up profits from room rentals. As such, only investors with previous restaurant experience should consider a hotel/restaurant combo.
- Hotels provide a far more fluid cash flow than other types of real estate, as tenants pay every day. However, your expenses will also be more fluid, with the need for daily maid service and frequent maintenance requests.

What do you want out of life?

If you make an incredible income, love your job, and want to continue living the way you are forever ... then perhaps real estate is not right for you. After all, real estate investing—no matter where it falls on the scale of passivity – is never completely painless. It does take work— even if that work is just mental. So if you don't want to improve, why get into real estate?

However, if you envision your future as something better than what you currently have, real estate investing can help. Now true – real estate is not the only way to build wealth.... In fact, given enough time, anyone can build serious wealth by just setting aside 20% of their paycheck and investing in low-risk mutual funds or stocks. Just ask Dave Ramsey.

However, my goal is not to retire in thirty years. Anyone can do that. My goal is to become financially free soon—to begin living a life defined not by a boss or by a job or financial constraints, but a life defined by choices; my choice.

Furthermore, real estate gives me the opportunity to build that financial freedom through multiple avenues. For example, for years I lived off the cash flow from my investments, but at the same time I allowed appreciation and the monthly loan pay-down to help my wealth grow while I sleep.

BRANDON TURNER
REAL-ESTATE INVESTOR AND SENIOR EDITOR OF BIGGERPOCKETS.COM

6

NARROWING THE FIELD

When a maxim keeps making the rounds for years, it must satisfy at least one of two criteria: (1) it's funny, or (2) it makes a point that never gets old. Perhaps the oldest maxim in the real estate business goes something like this:

Question: "What are the three most important factors in determining the value of a piece of property?"
Answer: "Location, location, location."

Based on your reading of chapter 5, which discussed the various types of rental property, you know this answer oversimplifies the situation. Plenty of other things matter, including economic trends, tenant selection, the building's condition, and most of all, cash flows.

But at heart, the maxim makes a valid point. Suppose you have the world's best office building, gleaming and new, packed with the latest amenities and a slate of top-flight tenants on 10-year leases. Drop that building on the corner of Wacker and Dearborn in Chicago's Loop, and you can sell it for nine figures. But if you instead plunk it down between a bank and a pet store on Main Street in a town in the Rust Belt, the price plummets.

Location has a huge effect on prices.

However, price doesn't mean *everything* when it comes to selecting an investment. Of course, anyone who has purchased a value meal at a fast-food joint instead of a five-course meal at a fancy restaurant already understands this phenomenon.

The fast-food meal may not measure up to the sit-down meal in quality, but the lower price you pay for the burger and fries reflects this disparity.

When you make the choice to purchase something rather than a possible substitute, you say something about the item's value relative to that substitute. Purchasing real estate works the same way.

Yes, pay attention to location. It matters too much to ignore.

Yes, pay attention to the building's price. Even the best property can be overpriced, and some pieces of real estate aren't worth the money even if you acquire them for free.

But don't let either location or price become the sole factor in deciding whether or not to make a real estate deal. You need to take both into account.

The Perfect Location

The perfect location doesn't exist. But that doesn't mean you should stop looking. To find the best rental property, try this seven-step process.

STEP 1 ▶ *Pick your poison*

By the time you finished chapter 5, you probably had an idea about which type of property would suit you. If not, go back and read the pros and cons for the major property types. Remember, beginning investors should probably stick to one of the following:

- Office
- Industrial
- Retail
- Multifamily

All four of these property groups delivered similarly solid returns from 1994 through 2009. Rather than try to pick which group will win over the next decade, decide on the type of property that appeals to you.

Feel free to select a second and third choice in case you can't find anything in the first group.

STEP 2 ▶ *Assess your area*

Real estate has many appeals as an investment, including the ability to purchase property anywhere in the country without leaving home. If you intend to hire someone else to manage your property, you don't need to live nearby or visit the place.

However, delegating all the management responsibilities to a third-party represents a risk, particularly for a first-time buyer. After all, can you really expect a hired manager to provide your building with the same care you'd give it?

At first blush, the preceding paragraph seems to conflict with earlier advice to consider a property manager. But consider the context. If you ran a business, would you hire a manager, then relax in a hot tub day after day and trust that manager to keep things going? Most real estate doesn't require the same level of oversight as a business with dozens of employees, but that doesn't mean you can simply stay home and collect checks. Particularly not for your first piece of property.

Experience really is the best teacher, and you'll learn more by getting your hands dirty. Even if you hire a property manager, you'll want to visit the site at least once a week to see what's happening.

Absentee landlords have trouble keeping up with developments related to their property. Experienced investors who have established a strong business relationship with a property manager can do just fine investing from a distance. But for your first (and probably second or third as well) real estate investment, stick closer to home and invest in an area you already know.

Before you focus on neighborhoods, take the pulse of your region. If you live near a city, focus on that city's metropolitan area. If you live in a sparsely populated area, set your sights a little wider, carving out a section of the state. Then consider a few key metrics that will help you judge both the health of the region and your best approach toward real estate investing.

- **Demographics.** Learn all you can about who lives and works in your target market. If possible, study segments of the market separately, as not every place will show the same trends. Regions with a high average age often have fewer families with children, which means you may have trouble renting large apartments. Areas inhabited by a high percentage of college graduates may see a greater need for office space.

    Find out the age, income level, and educational attainment of your target market. Demographics will help you determine what kind of retail tenants you want and the types of multifamily housing in greatest demand. *Sources:* The U.S. Census Bureau (www.census.gov) provides a wealth of information on regional and local demographics. Other useful tools include city-data.com and Google searches of a ZIP code.

- **Growth.** How fast has the population grown in the last year? The last five years? And which segments of the population are growing? Areas with high population growth should see more need for multifamily housing, and retail tends to follow multifamily. *Sources:* Try the Census Bureau as well as the websites of local and state governments or the Chamber of Commerce.

- **Labor.** If possible, you should invest in areas with lower-than-average unemployment. High unemployment could reflect a poor-quality workforce, a loss of businesses that employ local residents, or simply economic malaise. Regardless of the reason for the unemployment, you'll have an easier time finding and keeping tenants in an economically healthy area. *Sources:* The Bureau of Labor Statistics (BLS, www.bls.gov) tracks employment for states and metropolitan areas. Compare your area to the rest of the country. Many municipalities or other entities will track unemployment for areas far smaller than the BLS does, and www.city-data.com also provides this information, though the accuracy of unemployment numbers broken down by ZIP code is difficult to verify. Search government websites or newspaper stories to find the best possible information.
- **Construction.** Seek out data on building permits, which will provide you with hints about future growth. If contractors in your region are putting up office and industrial buildings and unemployment isn't too high, there's a good chance that demand for multifamily space will rise after companies move into those buildings and begin to hire. Of course, if housing (single-family or apartments) is going up in a region with little business growth, you may be seeing advance signs of overbuilding.

  Realize that none of these data points will tell you much by itself. But taken in concert, knowledge of construction trends, unemployment, and demographics will provide a fairly accurate picture of your community. *Sources:* Start with local government websites. Try planning or zoning boards. Most cities or counties will track this data. You just need to find it.
- **Household size.** This data point matters more to multifamily investors, but owners of other types of rental property can also benefit from such information. For instance, if the average size of a household in the city is 2.8 people versus 4.5 in the suburbs, you can understand why a building full of one-bedroom apartments downtown might have a lower vacancy rate than one in the suburbs. And what if you own retail space? A babyGap will probably do better in a region with 4.5 people per home than in one with 2.8 people per home. *Sources:* The Census Bureau tracks household data. For a tighter focus on a city or neighborhood, visit www.city-data.com.
- **Businesses.** This information may be tougher to pin down, but an investor should take the time to seek it out. Collect the names of the largest businesses in the area you target, and you'll get an idea of the type of workforce, and possibly other businesses likely to locate nearby. Learn the most common occupations of the people in your target market and you can better assess the business breakdown. *Sources:* The Census Bureau's American Community Survey and Economic Census can help, providing data at the state, county, city, town, or ZIP code level. You can also find plenty of useful information at www.city-data.com.

- **Occupancy rates.** Occupancy matters for a variety of reasons. Of course, the higher your occupancy, the greater your cash flows. But before you can assess an individual building, you must learn about the broader market. Has the square footage available for lease risen or fallen over the last year? How long has space remained on the market? Review this information for your chosen city, plus others nearby. Focus not just on the absolute numbers, but also on the trends. *Sources:* LoopNet.com offers a Market Trends feature that identifies the number of spaces available and square footage available (supply metrics) as well as the number of people looking for information on property and the length of time that space remains on the market (demand metrics). Your real estate agent may have access to more specific occupancy numbers.

- **Average rents.** This one sounds obvious, but too many investors don't take the time to do the research. If industrial space in your city rents for an average of $8 per square foot per year and the building you're eyeing charges only $6 per square foot, you may have the opportunity to raise rents. Alternatively, if the place demands $10 per square foot, you may have just learned why the building is half empty. *Sources:* LoopNet.com's Market Trends feature provides asking rents as well as actual rents for leased space, broken down by city. Your real estate agent should also be able to help with this.

Don't pin your hopes on a particular neighborhood, or even a particular type of property, until you've assessed the condition of your target market. You may have your heart set on owning high-end office space. But if your region contains mostly high school graduates and tends to attract industrial businesses, you may not find what you seek. And if you do find it, you may regret buying it.

Remember the adage about the square peg in the round hole? You can't change your market, and if you try to go against the area's grain, you'll create a lot of extra work for yourself. However, if you do a good job of determining what makes that market tick, you can identify a slice of that market and slide into a profitable property.

STEP 3 ▶ *Select your site*

Once you've got a handle on your target market, tighten your focus. At this stage, don't worry about exact addresses, just narrow down your preference to an area large enough to allow for some selection. For instance:

- If you want to buy an office property, determine where in the city or county or region businesses are locating. The archives of your local newspaper's business section can help with that. Look for news about deals or new space under construction. If you can find an office area fairly near a residential area with a growing population, so much the better.

- Looking for retail? Start with shopping centers or strip malls that see a steady stream of traffic and have full parking lots. Give precedence to locations with big-name anchors and a variety of types of stores. Aside from avoiding neighborhoods where you'll feel the need to bar the door or hire a security guard, don't worry too much about the socioeconomic level. You can make good money in lower-middle-class neighborhoods, just as you can in upper-class areas.
- Industrial investors should familiarize themselves with the layout of their region. You may have lived in a community all your life without visiting the industrial areas. Remedy that lack immediately. Drive through your town's industrial section (if it has one) and some industrial parks in various parts of town. If some look run-down or have more vacant buildings than others, find out why. Here again, the newspaper is a good resource.
- Unless you routinely drive all over residential areas, you may have a tough time doing advance location research for multifamily. Apartment complexes don't always locate in obvious areas, and depending on the composition of the neighborhood, there may be buildings with 4 to 12 units tucked between single-family homes. As with retail, avoid truly depressed areas, which add risk to any investment. If possible, try a middle-income area, as no matter what happens to the economy, plenty of middle-income people will still need a place to live.

You'll find a wide range of building sizes and prices. At this stage, you probably don't have enough information to arrange financing. But you can set a rough price range. Assume that you'll be able to borrow with a loan-to-value (LTV) ratio of 70 percent to 80 percent. If you have $50,000 to spend on a down payment, don't look at property that costs more than $250,000. In fact, set your sights lower than that so you can retain some cash to cover expenses.

How did $50,000 in cash translate to a $250,000 property? Subtract the LTV (80 percent) from 100 percent, and you have 20 percent, which tells you how much down payment you need. Divide your down payment ($50,000) by 20 percent, and you end up with $250,000.

The same tools you used to analyze your broad region can usually help you drill down to more granular data for your county or town, or even neighborhood. This information, coupled with any personal observations of the areas in question, should help you select a few choice locations for the type of property you wish to own.

STEP 4 ▶ *See what's available*

Start your search online, just as you would if you were looking for a new home. Some of the larger home-search websites also offer listings for commercial property. The quantity and quality of those listings vary, so visit as many as you need. See the "Online Options" box to get started.

ONLINE OPTIONS

If you're on the hunt for commercial property, start with the following national sites listed here. The list is far from comprehensive, and you may find a regional site that focuses on your area, particularly if you seek to purchase rental real estate in a major city.

- LoopNet.com claims to be the largest online commercial listing service. A search of Los Angeles found 456 buildings, with the promise of many more for a paid subscription.
- CoStar.com also claims to be the largest online commercial listing service and yielded more than 1,400 listings for Los Angeles.
- Realtor.com, the site administered by the National Association of Realtors, is best known for its home listings. However, as of January 1, 2013, the site featured 375 properties for sale in Los Angeles, ranging from vacant land to a $4.6 million office building on Wilshire Boulevard.
- Coldwell Banker Commercial (www.cbcworldwide.com) and Trulia.com don't feature as many investment properties as you'll find at Realtor.com, but they're worth checking.

While you should start your search online, the computer won't get you all the way there. The real estate sites don't seem to capture investment property as efficiently as they do homes, mostly because many commercial buildings never get listed with agents. With that in mind, it's time for the next step.

STEP 5 ▶ *Assemble your team*

After you've done some initial research online, find a commercial broker. While commercial real estate requires different contacts and some specialized knowledge, at its core the business operates much like residential real estate. As such, you should seek a commercial broker the same way you'd look for a residential broker:

- Personal referrals. If you know someone who has bought or sold commercial property, ask for a recommendation.
- Realtor.com. The National Association of Realtors website features a database of more than 1 million agents.
- National real estate brokerages. Coldwell Banker and Century 21 are two examples.

Target someone who focuses primarily on commercial property. Plenty of residential agents can do commercial deals, but they may not know as much about the ins and outs of commercial real estate, and they probably don't have the contacts needed to find the best properties and shepherd you through the purchasing process.

You may be thinking that you could save a few bucks by avoiding the agent and handling the purchase yourself. Well, you might, and you might not.

12 QUESTIONS TO ASK YOUR REAL ESTATE AGENT

Don't rush to hire the first real estate agent you meet. After all, you may end up paying this person thousands of dollars, so take the time to make sure you'll get your money's worth. To separate the wheat from the chaff, interview your agent before you make a decision. If the agent won't answer the following questions, you don't need to go any further.

1. **Do you handle real estate full-time?** Plenty of part-timers can get the job done, but agents who buy and sell real estate for a living probably know more about the market.

2. **How much of your business is commercial?** Can you do a profitable rental real estate deal with an agent who spends most of her time on residential property? Sure. But the residential and commercial markets don't travel the same paths, and familiarity counts.

3. **Do you have access to market data, such as occupancy and rental rates?** Consider this a back-door strategy for repeating question 2. Plenty of commercial developers and brokers gather data on occupancy. But with a few exceptions, you can't access it for free. A true expert in commercial real estate should have sufficient contacts to obtain this information for you.

4. **What do you charge?** Just as with residential real estate, the seller should pay the commission, with his agent receiving half (normally 3 percent) and your agent receiving the other half.

5. **How many deals have you done in my target market?** Give extra consideration to prospective agents who have bought or sold buildings similar to those that interest you and in the same area.

6. **Have any of your clients filed complaints against you?** Ask the question, record the answer, and then verify the answer with the agent's state licensing board.

7. **When clients aren't satisfied with your service, what went wrong?** Agents won't like to answer this, but the best ones should be up front about any issue. And by learning where the agent/client relationship broke down, you can assess whether you're likely to encounter the same troubles.

8. **What services do you offer?** The agent should handle paperwork, negotiate on your behalf, and help you deal with any legal issues that crop up.

9. **Do you represent both buyers and sellers for the same property?** This issue inspires a lot of passion in real estate agents, some in support and some opposed. However, since part of making the deal involves negotiating prices to obtain the best deal, it's tough to accept that an agent representing both sides of the transaction truly has your best interest at heart.

12 QUESTIONS TO ASK YOUR REAL ESTATE AGENT

(continued from previous page)

10. **Can you show me properties that aren't listed online?** Quality agents should know where to look for properties that suit your needs, even those represented by agents who don't use listing services or are for sale by owner.

11. **What sets you apart from other agents?** At this point you're looking for experience and knowledge. Passion and excitement are useful, but you're talking about real money. Stick with a veteran.

12. **Can I have references for your last five deals?** If you ask for a single reference, an agent can always pull out someone who likes him. But when you ask for five consecutive deals, you have a greater chance of unearthing someone with a negative story. Of course, if you just hear glowing reviews, you've probably found an agent who does a consistently good job.

Source: Redfin.com

Investors hire real estate agents for a lot of reasons other than arranging showings and preparing the closing documents. By spending some time and effort to select the best possible agent, you can avoid performing some of the riskiest and most difficult tasks yourself.

For instance, many real estate books devote large sections to negotiating deals. However, most of you should let your agent do the dirty work. Remember, it shouldn't cost you any more to hire a truly great agent than you'd spend on an average agent. So find the best you can, someone who can advise you on the financing process, help you pick out property, and strike the hardest bargain.

Once you retain an agent, start narrowing down your list of properties. You'll do this taking into account your agent's expertise, your own time constraints (after all, you need to tour all these sites), and the analysis tools presented in chapter 7.

In addition to an agent, you should find an accountant who can help you analyze the financial data you'll receive from the property owner. The numbers aren't rocket science, and most accountants can provide the insight you need.

Many experts also advise hiring a lawyer, one versed in real estate, to negotiate with the seller and/or the lender and to prepare your purchase contract. Depending on the confidence you have in your real estate agent, you may not require a lawyer's negotiation services. As for the contract, we provide a sample on page 109 to give you a general idea of what to expect. Many public-domain contracts are available online, and you can customize them to suit your needs.. However, if the idea of using a public-domain contract concerns you, pay the lawyer for peace of mind.

The last member of your team is the lender or mortgage broker, who warrants his own step.

STEP 6 ▶ *Arrange your financing*

Commercial real estate transactions tend to take longer than home sales, mostly because of the financing, so you should start working on your loan early.

So why isn't this step 1? Because until you have a good idea of the type of property you wish to buy, commercial lenders won't help you that much. Bankers tend to treat commercial mortgages like business loans, considering more than just the value of the real estate when making decisions.

Keep in mind that an individual seeking to buy her first piece of rental real estate may not look like a good risk, particularly to a bank. Most banks underwriting a commercial mortgage will expect the borrower to possess resources other than the property, and even then the loan will cost more than a home loan of similar size. Don't expect a 30-year term, and do expect a serious credit check.

If you don't have top-notch credit and a demonstrable ability to pay down at least part of the loan *without* drawing on the real estate's cash flows, a bank loan may not work for you. Many—perhaps most—first-time real estate investors won't have enough documentation to satisfy banks' expectations.

Nonbank lenders often require less stringent terms, allowing smaller down payments and longer loan periods—at the cost of a higher interest rate. However, just because you can borrow at an 85 percent LTV doesn't mean you should. Remember the earlier discussion of how cash flows on real estate can turn negative? High borrowing costs exacerbate that problem, while the more leverage you use, the bigger your risk of loss if the deal goes sour.

And don't forget—after you borrow, set some cash aside to cover unexpected expenses or shortfalls.

Commercial mortgages often require covenants, promises that go beyond paying off the loan on time. The lender could require that you provide frequent financial updates or meet minimum cash-flow targets, among other things.

Many commercial mortgages also carry prepayment penalties, which prevent you from paying off the loan early, even if you sell the property. Some loans, however, will allow the purchaser to assume the mortgage. Such loans should make the selling process easier and faster by providing the buyer with a direct link to financing.

An experienced real estate agent can probably help you navigate the loan process. But even in an environment of low interest rates, commercial lending takes longer and entails more hassles than a residential loan. Most local banks and commercial lenders can handle loans of up to $1 million or more, so you should have options.

If you plan to purchase your real estate with cash on hand, skip this step. Cash buyers can do their deals much more quickly than those using mortgages.

STEP 7 ▶ *Visit your prospects*

Never buy investment property without touring the site.

That instruction is worth repeating, with emphasis: *Never buy investment property without touring the site.*

If you don't live near the property, either take the time to make the journey or target something closer to home. When you have 10 profitable deals under your belt and a network of contacts you can trust, then go ahead and buy sight unseen if you must. But commercial real estate entails risk even for investors who do their homework. The less up-front work you do, the more risk you invite.

During the tour, take the time you need to inspect potential trouble spots. Even if you don't know anything about plumbing, check out the pipes and fixtures and take photos of anything that looks suspicious. If you have a friend, relative, or partner who knows more about construction and renovation than you do, bring him along.

Yes, you'll have the chance to perform a detailed inspection later on. But a small expenditure of time up front could save you a lot of time and money by ruling out troublesome properties before you make an offer.

Some owners will balk at your request to tour the property. They might say the tenants will get upset or claim they can't get you in. Just let them know that having no access to the property is a deal breaker. Many a property owner has purchased a building with an attractive façade only to find out that it will take $100,000 in renovations to make the place habitable.

Never forget that these deals mean real money. View the property in person before you commit. And if you can pay a reasonable fee to have an expert accompany you on this visit, do it. If you perform the walk-through alone, take copious notes and photos. If possible, review them with an expert before you make an offer.

You can assess one important aspect of any building without outside help: Always check out the parking. Far too many buildings lack sufficient parking for their tenants and customers.

If you can, walk around the neighborhood and acquaint yourself with other businesses in the area.

After completing the seven steps, you have hopefully assembled a small list of prospects—all properties you feel excited about owning, all in neighborhoods with potential.

To choose among those hot options, turn to the numbers. In some cases, the seller will share a few of his cash-flow numbers and other operating data before you make an offer to purchase. If so, take everything you can get and pore over it with your accountant. However, you might have nothing more than the rental and vacancy rates and property tax information. Fortunately, you can do a lot with just a little data, as you'll learn in chapter 7.

Real estate developers have long understood that ground-up construction isn't necessarily the best solution. In dense urban areas with an abundance of aging inventory, underperforming buildings (I'm thinking of high-rise office, apartment, and hotel assets in particular) may offer more value than a ground-up development. Consider landmark properties like the Empire State Building, whose landlord . . . invested enormous amounts of money into renovating and modernizing. Of course, not every aging or landmark property comes with the Empire State Building's prestige, but still, a lot of these assets offer incredible value to owners, operators, and tenants.

Recently, many cities have seen a great number of instances in which aging office properties are repositioned as luxury condos or other such multifamily properties. This, of course, has been a fortuitous situation since office demand for C and B-class office real estate has diminished since the Great Recession, with only Class A properties in CBDs able to attract a suitable occupancy. Office fundamentals have improved since the recession, and I attribute much of this situation to the fact that there is less aging office inventory on the market and inflating the national and local vacancy rates.

ERIC HAWTHORN
LLENROCK GROUP

7

JUST THE RIGHT SITE

Now you're cooking. You've identified your target market, highlighting a few neighborhoods or areas of particular appeal. With the help of your real estate agent, you've narrowed down the list, then visited the sites personally, and narrowed it down some more. At this stage, you should have fewer than five hot prospects. But what if you still love them all?

Maybe you don't really love every one of them. However, if you're like most people, you'll take a shine to more than one.

Any experienced investor will tell you that you can't buy everything that strikes your fancy. Unless you set unrealistic expectations or limit yourself to a tiny geographic area, the number of properties out there that could make money for you will exceed your ability to purchase them.

The last stage of the process, the last step before you make the offer, requires some number crunching. But don't panic. The math is pretty simple.

Involve your accountant if you like. But anyone who owns a calculator, uses a spreadsheet program, or graduated high school with a C+ in math can handle the step-by-step process detailed in the next few pages.

Establishing the Value

As you prepare to run the numbers, keep the following three concepts in mind. You probably didn't learn any of them in high school.

1. When professional investors value an asset, they don't stop at the price. A $100,000 property isn't necessarily cheaper than a $500,000 property. *Valuation* considers the price relative to income or cash flows. If the $100,000 property generates $10,000 in annual cash flows (price/cash flow ratio of $100,000 over $10,000, or 10) and the $500,000 property delivers $65,000 in cash flows (price/cash flow ratio of $500,000 over $65,000, or 7.7), which is cheaper?

2. Asset values vary based on the perspective of the person with the calculator. This isn't 2 + 2 = 4. Valuation relies on a lot of assumptions about what will happen in the future, and you and your banker might have different views on a property's worth.

3. The very act of investing entails risk, so don't compound that risk by making bad guesses. When in doubt, be conservative. When you make calculations, act as if your property will face higher vacancy rates, larger renovation expenses, and tougher economic conditions than you really expect. If a property looks good using conservative assumptions, you may have a winner.

A caveat: If you must repair or renovate a property immediately after purchase to make it suitable for your purposes, include those costs in the purchase price when preparing your cash-flow analysis. If you spend $500,000 for a building and immediately sink $100,000 into a new electrical and heating system, then you'll want to compare your cash flows to an investment of $600,000, not $500,000.

Armed with these concepts, you're ready to crunch some numbers. And so is Pete Property, who just finished the book you're reading right now. He has $500,000 to invest and can borrow at an LTV of 75 percent. Pete has culled the herd down to three properties, all located in Rentland, a suburb of Chicago:

- A five-story brownstone with two apartments on each floor. Asking price: $1.1 million.
- A 15,000-square-foot professional building with three units. Asking price: $2 million.
- A mini strip mall with six storefronts, each with 3,000 square feet of space. Asking price: $950,000.

Most sellers will provide buyers with just enough information to get them interested in the property. Fortunately, you can estimate or extrapolate most of the numbers for your cash-flow report. But in order to analyze a property, you need at least two pieces of information:

- The size and rental rates of the units.
- The costs to operate the property.

If the seller won't provide the first piece of information, eliminate that property in the first stage of your analysis. Some will provide data on costs before you make an offer, some won't. Use what they give you and estimate the rest.

PETE'S CASH-FLOW ANALYSIS, STEP 1			
	Brownstone multifamily	**Professional building**	**Strip mall**
Rentable units	10 apartments, each with two bedrooms, 1,200 square feet	Three offices, each 5,000 square feet	Three units, total of 9,000 square feet
Asking price	$1,100,000	$2,000,000	$950,000
Down payment	$500,000	$500,000	$500,000
Loan-to-value	55%	75%	47%
Loan needed (30 years at 6%)	$600,000	$1,500,000	$450,000
Rentable square feet	12,000	**15,000**	**9,000**
Rentable units	**10**	3	3
Annual rent	$18,000 per unit	$17 per square foot	$15 per square foot
ANNUAL INCOME			
Gross potential income	**$180,000**	**$255,000**	**$135,000**
Allowance for vacancy	5%	6%	6%
Real potential income	**$171,000**	**$242,250**	**$128,250**
ANNUAL OPERATING EXPENSES			
Property taxes	$17,000	$32,500	$14,000
Insurance	$12,000	$9,000	$11,000
Services (trash collection, landscaping, snow removal)	$18,000	$4,000	$4,000
Utilities (gas, electric, water)	$0	$15,000	$11,000
Maintenance	$16,500	$10,000	$14,250
Property management	$0	$7,000	$4,000
Unit for on-site superintendent	$18,000	$0	$0
Operating expenses	**$81,500**	**$77,500**	**$58,250**
Net operating income	**$89,500**	**$164,750**	**$70,000**
Capitalization rate	**8.1%**	**8.2%**	**7.4%**
Renovation reserves	$11,000	$30,000	$9,500
Debt service (mortgage)	$43,168	$107,919	$32,376
Before-tax cash flow	**$35,332**	**$26,831**	**$28,124**
Cash-on-cash return	**7.1%**	**5.4%**	**5.6%**

All three of Pete's prospective sellers claimed the buildings were fully leased. He visited the properties and verified that the office and retail spaces had tenants, but couldn't get an accurate count at the apartment brownstone.

Pete knows he can't truly capture all of the costs until he gets a closer look at the owner's financials—which won't happen until he makes an offer. But he's prepared a cash-flow analysis on all three properties, as shown in the preceding Step 1 table.

Some of the information Pete already knew, some he collected, and some he estimated. When you buy a property, create a sheet similar to this one. Line by line, here's how Pete did it. Pay attention, because while your property will give you different numbers, you'll want to prepare your own sheet in much the same way.

- **Down payment:** To limit his borrowing, Pete assumed he'd use his $500,000 as a down payment. That starting point showed him how much he had to borrow.
- **Rent:** The sellers provided information on square footage and rental rates.
- **Gross potential income:** Pete calculated gross potential income assuming the space was 100 percent leased.
- **Vacancy allowance:** Many investors use 5 percent as a proxy for vacancy, but Pete's real estate agent obtained average vacancy rates for Rentland, so Pete used those. Subtracting the vacancy allowance from gross potential income yielded real potential income.
- **Property taxes:** One of the sellers provided this data, and Pete obtained the other two numbers from the local assessor.
- **Insurance, services, and utilities:** Pete spent a couple hours on the phone to get quotes. They're estimates, but probably not too far from actual expenses.
- **Maintenance:** A common industry standard estimate is 1 percent of the property value. To be conservative, Pete assumed 1.5 percent of the asking price, which is more than he expects to pay.
- **Property management and superintendant:** The multifamily unit has a super who rents out apartments and does simple maintenance in exchange for free rent. For the other two properties, Pete called three property managers and averaged their price quotes.
- **Net operating income:** This is just real potential income minus operating expenses.
- **Capitalization rate (cap rate):** A common measurement of value, the *capitalization rate* is the net operating income divided by the property's value, in this case estimated by the asking price. Higher is better, and all three of these cap rates exceed the national average for similar properties. However, while the cap rate is a popular metric, it has two weaknesses. First, it relies on the property value, which is always subjective. Second, it doesn't take leverage into account.
- **Renovation reserves:** Pete intends to set money aside for the inevitable renovations. He can't predict his needs, but 1 percent of the building's asking price seems like a good start. During his initial tour, the multifamily and retail properties looked

to be in good shape, but the office complex badly needed new windows, and its furnace looked quite old. So the office reserves are 1.5 percent of the asking price.

- **Debt service:** Pete relied on a mortgage calculator, based on a 30-year mortgage at 6 percent. He plans to use a commercial lender that will give him a long-term loan.
- **Before-tax cash flow:** This is the net operating income minus renovation reserves and debt service.
- **Cash-on-cash return:** This is the after-tax cash flow divided by Pete's down payment, the amount of money he plans to put at risk. For most real estate investors, cash-on-cash return is the real bottom line.

Cash-flow analysis done, Pete must now answer two questions:

- Should he purchase any of these real estate investments?
- If he makes an offer, which one should he try to buy?

Is It Time to Buy?

This is quite literally the million-dollar question, and the answer depends on more than just the cash-flow analysis. To make this decision, Pete must assess the investment's *opportunity cost*.

Every time you spend money to purchase something, you sacrifice all the other items you might have bought instead. Consider them lost opportunities. Thus, the concept of opportunity cost. If, by making an investment, you miss out on the chance to earn a similar return with less risk or a higher return with similar risk, then the opportunity cost of your investment is probably too high.

Suppose Pete can purchase a long-term corporate bond mutual fund—essentially buying interest payments on a company's debt—that pays a 5 percent yield, well below the cash-on-cash return of the multifamily building and slightly below those of the office and retail properties. However, while the NCREIF Property Index has historically been less volatile than long-term corporate bonds as a broad class of assets, the typical bond fund carries substantially less risk than the typical piece of real estate.

Back in the introduction, you learned that from 1978 through 2012, real estate delivered total returns slightly below those of long-term bonds, taking into account both the income and the capital gains. However, from 1994 through 2009, all five of the major real estate classes managed annual returns of at least 12 percent, well above the return of bonds. Will those robust returns repeat? Tough to tell, and there's the rub.

Higher Return Potential, Higher Risk

To compensate for the extra risk, Pete would prefer a cash-on-cash return of 10 percent. At minimum, he'll demand a return of 7.5 percent—half again what he could bring in with a bond. None of the properties meet that target, but the apartments come close, with a 7.1 percent return.

Pete made a point of using conservative estimates for maintenance and reno-vation costs, and he believes he can earn higher returns than his cash-flow analysis suggests. In addition, he expects to pay less than the asking price for his building, which should lower his financing costs. But that conservatism should have built in some insulation from market downturns, and relaxing those assumptions simply to make the deal look better would defeat the purpose.

Even using a conservative view, Pete appreciates the potential returns of the real estate. In addition, he could benefit from the diversification because he already owns stocks and bonds. Perhaps he can still achieve his target return, either by cutting operating expenses or negotiating a lower price on the building.

Pete decides to buy a piece of property, but commits to walking away unless the cash-on-cash return reaches 7.5 percent.

That leaves just one question: Which building should he buy?

Adjusting the Picture

By the numbers, the multifamily property is obviously the best, right? It offers a 7.1 percent cash-on-cash return if Pete's assumptions about income and expenses hold out. And Pete can purchase the property at a substantially lower LTV than the office building, which suggests less risk.

But the numbers can lie. Pete's cash-flow analysis depends heavily on assump-tions, just like yours will. Before committing so much money, he decides to go through the data again. Some numbers, like square footage and property taxes, are what they are. However, an investor may have the power to make changes and alter some of the assumptions to improve his odds of making a profit.

Before you finalize your cash-flow analysis, consider three potential areas where you can make changes:

- **Financing.** Can you raise more cash for the down payment? Have you shopped around to obtain the best interest rate? If Pete could borrow at 5 percent rather than 6 percent, he could reduce his annual mortgage expense for the office build-ing by more than $11,000. That would boost the cash-on-cash return to 7.6 percent from 5.4 percent. However, Pete has shopped around, and he can't do better than 6 percent.

- **Income.** Don't give in to the temptation to reduce your vacancy allowance. Yes, you might be able to keep occupancy higher than the target level. Then again, you might not. Don't nibble around the edges to smooth out your numbers.

   Rental rates are another matter. A few phone calls to other apartment com-plexes tells Pete that for two-bedroom units, $1,500 per month is the going rate. However, some additional research reveals that while the office property's rental

PETE'S CASH-FLOW ANALYSIS, STEP 2			
	Brownstone multifamily	**Professional building**	**Strip mall**
Rentable units	10 apartments, each with two bedrooms, 1,200 square feet	Three offices, each 5,000 square feet	Three units, total of 9,000 square feet
Asking price	$1,100,000	$2,000,000	$950,000
Down payment	$500,000	$500,000	$500,000
Loan-to-value	55%	75%	47%
Loan needed (30 years at 6%)	$600,000	$1,500,000	$450,000
Rentable square feet	12,000	**15,000**	**9,000**
Rentable units	**10**	3	3
Annual rent	$18,000 per unit	$17 per square foot	$18 per square foot
ANNUAL INCOME			
Gross potential income	**$180,000**	**$255,000**	**$162,000**
Allowance for vacancy	5%	6%	6%
Real potential income	**$171,000**	**$242,250**	**$153,900**
ANNUAL OPERATING EXPENSES			
Property taxes	$17,000	$32,500	$14,000
Insurance	$12,000	$9,000	$11,000
Services (trash collection, landscaping, snow removal)	$18,000	$4,000	$4,000
Utilities (gas, electric, water)	$0	$15,000	$11,000
Maintenance	$24,000	$10,000	$14,250
Property management	$0	$0	$0
Unit for on-site superintendent	$0	$0	$0
Operating expenses	**$71,000**	**$70,500**	**$54,250**
Net operating income	**$100,000**	**$171,750**	**$99,650**
Capitalization rate	**9.1%**	**8.6%**	**10.5%**
Renovation reserves	$11,000	$30,000	$9,500
Debt service (mortgage)	$43,168	$107,919	$32,376
Before-tax cash flow	**$45,832**	**$33,831**	**$57,774**
Cash-on-cash return	**9.2%**	**6.8%**	**11.6%**

rates match the city average, retail property charges an average of $18 per square foot per year, versus the $15 the mini strip mall charges. His real estate agent checks out the price of nearby retail space and suggests Pete could raise the rental rate to the city average and still attract tenants.

- **Expenses.** A line-by-line review of each expense category takes time. And if you can increase the profitability of your investment, you'll be glad you invested that time. Pete reviews his expense assumptions and finds them both reasonable and conservative. But near the bottom of the section, he spots a few ways to cut costs.

  First, he could manage the office or retail properties himself and save the $4,000 per year on the retail property or $7,000 for the professional building. Is the extra cash worth the hassle of handling tenant interactions and leasing? There's no right answer; it depends on the investor's preference. Pete, who has managed property in the past, decides he'd rather have the cash.

  Second, Pete could stop providing free lodging for the superintendent and manage the place himself, admittedly a more time-consuming venture than managing the professional or retail buildings. He can handle everything the super did except the repairs, which calls for an increase in his estimate for maintenance costs. As you'll learn in chapter 8, this strategy isn't for everyone.

The preceding Step 2 table illustrates what happens when Pete alters his assumptions. The changes make all three properties more appealing, but raising the retail rental rates caused the biggest bump, boosting the cash-on-cash return to 11.6 percent from 5.6 percent.

After his second take on the cash-flow analysis, Pete's path is clear. Both the retail building and the apartments satisfy his requirement for 7.5 percent cash-on-cash returns. However, the retail deal stands out, providing the superior return while requiring the smallest loan.

Of course, your journey will throw you different twists than Pete's. But the process remains the same:

- First, use conservative assumptions when creating your cash-flow sheet.
- Second, take the time needed to call around so you can use the most accurate estimates.
- Third, consider alternative investment options. Take into account diversification, as well as risk and potential returns.
- Fourth, set the deal aside for a day or two, and then review your work and revisit every line of the analysis.

Complete those steps in order, and you'll know whether to buy and what to target when the time is right.

Next up—doing the deal.

WHAT TENANTS WANT

The demands of office and industrial tenants are constantly changing. However, in recent years the transformations have come more quickly than usual. Here is what today's renters—particularly companies that employ younger workers—expect from their space:

- **Efficiency and productivity.** While tycoons like Donald Trump still profit from the desire for trophy buildings, most tenants can't afford that kind of space and instead focus on different objectives. In the wake of the Great Recession, businesses have renewed their focus on cutting costs and doing more with less. While some companies have reverted to the old ways as their prospects improved, plenty have hewed to the "lean and mean" management style.

- **Flexibility.** The preceding point flows into a second expectation: freedom to adapt the space to suit a particular company's needs. In a middle-market building, look for property with open-plan office space and efficient design. Today's flexible cubicle layouts allow employers to pack a lot of workers into a small space. If your building also provides some gathering points for social interaction, many tenants will consider it a plus.

- **High-tech amenities.** Top-of-the-line communications and a robust data center will go further than vaulted ceilings and corner offices in attracting tenants. Have people lost their interest in frills? Not at all. But fewer businesses will pay up for massive picture windows and plush carpeting these days.

- **Comfortable work environment.** The echo boomers and Generation Y, who make up the core of the workforce and make an increasing amount of America's business decisions, expect a higher quality of life at the workplace than baby boomers did. Many of them prefer a green approach, with energy-efficient systems and soft, natural-looking light.

Source: 2013 Emerging Trends in Real Estate

Making the Buy

Many sales professionals will tell you negotiation is the fun part. And maybe for them it is. Just don't kid yourself. Unless you revel in the art of the deal, unless you're the type of person who usually wins verbal disputes, argues down prices in department stores, and finishes poker games with the largest stack of chips, you probably won't win this fight. That's why you assembled a team. If you haven't hired a real estate agent or a lawyer who can negotiate better than you can, then you've missed the point.

FROM OFFER TO OWNERSHIP

Once you make an offer on a piece of property, the wheels of a complex process begin to turn. Here is a typical timeline.

- **The offer.** Don't offer a dime unless you've identified both your target price and the top of your range. Then start below your target and see how the seller responds. Never let anyone—either on your team or the seller's—rush you into a decision. When someone threatens to walk away from the deal if you don't sign this week, let them walk. Most of the time, they won't. In your letter of intent (see page 105 for a sample), be sure to request data on leases, service contracts, rental information that includes security deposits and current payments, insurance policies, and at least two years of financial statements and tax bills.

- **The contract.** After you strike a deal, you'll submit a contract like the one on page 107. Your contract should establish at least 30 days for due diligence, as well as access to all files and records. Be sure to set a date when the money becomes "hard," which means your earnest money is no longer refundable if you back out.

- **Due diligence.** The phrase due diligence refers to the level of care reasonable people take before entering into a financial transaction. During the due diligence period, you and your accountant should review the seller's financial documents. At this point you can adjust your income and expense numbers if needed to reflect actual costs rather than your estimates.

  Order an appraisal (expect it to take three to four weeks and cost several times as much as a residential appraisal) and inspections. When in doubt, go heavy on the inspections, looking at the interior, roof, air-conditioning, plumbing, and electrical. If the property needs renovations, get an estimate from two or three contractors so you can build the cost into your cash-flow model. Start the permitting process for any property improvements.

  All these services will cost you several thousand dollars. That's one of the reasons why you should do all the analysis you can before making an offer. In some cases, due diligence takes longer than the contract allows, which puts your earnest money at risk. You can take steps to finish your due diligence quickly, but a real estate investor should always be prepared to lose his earnest money.

- **Renegotiation.** Your financial analysis and inspections may reveal information that renders the property less valuable. Drawing on that information, restart the negotiation process. If you reach this point before the money goes hard, you can still back out without eating anything beyond the cost of your due diligence.

- **Hard money period.** After your due diligence deadline passes, you may have to chip in more earnest money.

- **Closing.** At this point, you take possession of the property and can begin to make improvements.

Once you've performed your cash-flow analysis and selected a target, determine the price you're willing to pay. If, like Pete, you've identified a property that meets or exceeds your investment goals at the asking price, then you should be willing to pay what the buyer wants. Of course, that doesn't prevent you from trying to knock the price down. In many cases, the deal will make sense only if you can buy for less than the asking price.

Only you can determine how much a piece of real estate is worth, because you'll be writing the check. Set a hard target above which you will not buy and a soft target that you'd prefer to pay; then consult with your agent and/or lawyer to start the process.

Purchasing investment property requires more work and more time than buying a home. Don't let the process intimidate you, but you shouldn't take it lightly. Many an investor has lost money by skipping steps.

Learn the process as well as you can. Every deal unfolds differently, though the sample timeline "From Offer to Ownership" outlines the major stages.

By this point you understand a lot more about property acquisition than you did before. But don't let that knowledge go to your head. You should know enough to ensure that the professionals you hired aren't leading you astray, but you probably don't know enough to do the job yourself without making rookie mistakes.

Once you've done your research, crunched the numbers, and taken aim at your target, trust your team to help your shot strike home.

If you've read through the list of steps and concluded that these will cost you some up-front money—congratulations, you got it right. The old phrase "It takes money to make money" applies with most types of investing, but never more than with real estate.

Your agent will get her cut when the deal goes down. But before you reach that point, you'll pay the inspectors and the appraiser, which again illustrates the reasons for setting some cash aside at the start of the process. The accountant helping with your due diligence won't work for free. And if you consulted him earlier in the process to assist with the cash-flow analysis, expect to pay a few hundred more.

Costs will vary based on the size of the property, the condition of the financial records, and the complexity of the inspections. Factor in closing costs, and you can expect to pay at least $5,000—probably more. When companies buy other companies, they often spend millions on due diligence—not because they're rolling in dough, but because the cost of getting it wrong is far higher.

Don't worry, your deal won't cost that much. But when you consider the dollars you'll commit to this purchase and the potential long-term revenue stream it provides, spending a few thousand on the front end makes sense.

Sometimes due diligence will unearth fixable problems you can leverage into a lower price. Sometimes it will bring to light ugly truths that cause you to walk away from the deal before you get soaked. And sometimes due diligence reveals nothing more than the fact that the building is just what it appears to be, giving you added confidence about the deal.

In all three of those situations, you've gotten your money's worth.

If you've come this far, don't balk at writing some checks. The Bible says a workman is worthy of his hire, and in this case, money truly can buy you peace of mind. It will also buy a wealth of knowledge and expertise. You can learn a lot from your team.

Observe your agent, lawyer, and accountant in action. Pay attention, ask questions, and pipe in with suggestions or even demands when you feel the urge. And at the end of the path, after you've become the proud owner of your first piece of rental property, you can smile, shake hands, and pay your experts.

Next time, you shouldn't require as much help.

But who are you kidding? You don't have time to think about another deal yet.

Congratulations on your property purchase. Now, in part 3 of this book, you'll learn how to manage it.

PART III

Managing Your Empire

I don't look at real estate as making a quick buck. I want to build beautiful buildings and leave something behind that will be remembered.

I knew it was for me. I had always dabbled in real estate. I love renovation, the construction side, the smell of concrete. It turns me on.

I didn't start with a lot of money. I started with a credit line and borrowed against two buildings of mine in Frankfurt. We were able to buy really great assets at great locations, at cheap prices. Then we hired great architects.

ABY ROSEN
NEW YORK REAL ESTATE MOGUL

8

BEING A LANDLORD

People cause a lot more trouble than numbers. Plenty of first-time real estate investors sweat the research or the data crunching or the due diligence, and with justification. None of that stuff is easy. However, books like this one can smooth out the process and provide you with the tools to make decisions.

By now, you should have a good handle on how the market for commercial real estate works and how to participate in it. You can determine which buildings you wish to buy, analyze those properties, and pick the best option. And you can take the steps needed to purchase that building.

But some lessons cannot truly be taught, only learned by experience. Which takes you to property management.

On the following pages you'll read about your responsibilities as a landlord. However, the actual process of managing a building—which, more than anything, revolves around managing people—can't be learned from a book.

Sure, you can pick up pointers. But despite the thousands of pages written about the subject, you won't truly understand property management until you've either tried it or spent a lot of time observing those who do it well.

Has anyone come up with the perfect line that any young man can use to persuade the cute lady down the street to go out with him? How about the strategy a worker can employ to wangle a raise out of a cranky boss? And what about the five steps any spouse can use to smooth out a rocky marriage?

They don't exist, because you can't count on two people reacting the same way to the same stimulus. And while you may classify tenants based on the unit they occupy, their business, or their lease terms, never forget that they are also people who will follow their own leanings.

No step-by-step process will make you an expert property manager. Consider managing property like nurturing a series of relationships with individuals, each different than the last. Then mix in a few variables, like the fact that some will leave without much warning, forcing you to bring in new blood.

Is the process really that complex? Not always. Most tenants won't require too much personal attention, and some would rather you just cash their check every month and leave them alone. But like any relationship, you must develop rapport with—or at least tolerance for—your tenants over time and adapt your actions based on how they react to different situations.

Don't worry too much. Expect to make mistakes at first, but you'll get better over time.

All that said, and acknowledging that no step-by-step process will get you all the way home, here's a seven-step process that will at least take you to the right neighborhood. And before you start reading, here's a hint: If you get step 1 right, all the others will become easier.

STEP 1 ▶ *Hire a property manager*

Give serious thought to paying someone to manage your first building, particularly if you purchase multifamily property, unless you fit the following criteria:

- Have worked in the property-management field.
- Possess the financial resources to recover from a few costly mistakes without putting the property in jeopardy.
- Can't make the deal work financially unless you manage the property yourself.

In fact, reason C might provide more justification for scrapping the deal than for shouldering those responsibilities. People generally tend to overestimate their abilities and underestimate the complexity of other people's jobs. That's why so many good cooks start restaurants, only to find that preparing tasty food doesn't ensure success.

It takes a lot of hubris to assume that you could read a book, peruse a few websites, and then jump in and manage property better than a professional. A part of you already understands this. Most people have the skill to change the oil in their car or even replace the brakes if they learn the basics. But if your transmission is shot, would you check out a few YouTube videos, then trust yourself to replace that key component in your car?

Of course not.

The last few paragraphs weren't meant to scare you. Well, maybe a little bit. Multifamily property, in particular, can get complicated because of the large number of tenants and their use of the property seven days a week, 24 hours a day.

WHAT TO EXPECT FROM YOUR MANAGER

You can pay your property manager a flat fee to handle everything if you like. Many owners will instead compensate for leasing separately. Regardless of how you arrange payment, expect the following from your manager:

- **Personal contact.** If you can't reach the person managing your property, then you've got the wrong person doing the job. You own the property, and the manager is working for you. Expect promptly returned phone calls, open communication, and a willingness to listen to your concerns and answer questions. Of course, you can make the relationship work more smoothly if you don't call and pester your manager every day.

- **Disclosure.** Let the property manager know you expect to hear about what's happening with the property. Arrange with her to provide you regular updates on the following:
  - Recurring tenant issues.
  - Cash-flow problems.
  - Inspections, including copies of any photographs taken.
  - Problems with the consistency or quality of work provided by any outside contractors.

- **Maintenance.** A competent property manager will handle most routine maintenance calls. A proactive manager will alert you if problems occur too often, or if she sees a need for preventive maintenance.

- **Prompt payments.** Before you hire the manager, iron out the details about when you will receive your rent checks.

- **Comprehensive service.** One of the reasons you hire a property manager—for most investors, the main reason—is so she can handle problems with tenants. Your manager should take the lead on any evictions, call tenants who violate the terms of their leases, and deal with unpleasant tenant conduct, such as damaging the property, causing trouble with other tenants, or failing to pay the rent. Let your property manager take point on these issues, but also tell her that you expect to be notified about such problems. If the situation gets ugly, don't hesitate to call in your lawyer; you hired him for these occasions, after all.

- **A buffer.** Hiring a property manager doesn't free you from all responsibility. But when you go with a professional manager or management company, you should expect to be contacted only when a serious problem occurs, or when the manager needs to pass on information you've requested. If the manager calls too often, find out why. Your property may simply require a lot of personal attention. But it's also possible that you've hired a manger who likes to delegate upward.

If you truly want to manage your own property, start out with something other than multifamily. But if possible, hire a property manager and see how it's done. Let the manager know up front that you intend to be involved, and don't hesitate to ask questions.

STEP 2 ▶ *Find a lawyer who knows the real estate business*

You may not need a lawyer during the purchase process. But once you own the property, legal assistance becomes a requirement rather than a luxury.

At some point a dispute will occur. Your tenants may already have their own attorneys, and all the insurance companies involved will certainly lawyer up. It's the old joke about bringing a knife to a gunfight.

Suppose your tenant, an architect, brings a client to the office for a meeting, and that client takes a nasty fall while walking into the conference room. Whose insurance will cover the costs?

If you own retail, office, or industrial property, having a lawyer may prove even more important than a property manager. This holds true regardless of the condition of the building or the diligence of management.

For instance, one property manager told of a mishap in which a second-floor office tenant failed to properly insulate a sprinkler, which malfunctioned and caused water damage in some retail space on the first floor. Each of the parties involved—the office tenant, the retail tenant, and the building owner—could make the argument that the other two bear responsibility. In such situations, you'll be glad to have a lawyer you can trust.

In the preceding case, the lawyers resolved the issue without taking it to court, though some disputes will go further. Regardless, you need a lawyer to represent your interest.

STEP 3 ▶ *Master the differences among property types*

Most office, industrial, and retail clients perform their own internal maintenance, like carpet cleaning. They'll also expect more freedom to remodel than apartment dwellers.

Multifamily properties will probably require consistent advertising and leasing activity, in addition to generating more calls and complaints. Not surprisingly, you'll pay more to hire a manager for your multifamily property than you would for another type of rental property of similar size.

STEP 4 ▶ *Learn your leases and your tenants*

Every property is different, and for the most part, the leases reflect those differences.

You should know the terms, covenants, and restrictions of every tenant lease. Never allow yourself to be surprised when a tenant's lease expires. If the term is coming to a close and the tenant hasn't brought up a renewal, ask him about his plans. The earlier you begin looking for new tenants, the less time your unit will sit vacant, generating no cash flow.

If possible, walk the property and meet the people who write the checks. As you read in chapter 5, in some cases the nature of their businesses will affect the overall health of the building.

A competent property manager will screen the tenants for you, and a competent owner will let her do the job. But by all means, get involved. Observe how the manager performs due diligence, and weigh in if you have questions or an opinion.

Depending on the condition and location of your building and the economic outlook, you won't always have options. However, when your property attracts more interest than you have space available, be picky and give precedence to tenants with the following characteristics:

- Viable businesses with large existing client bases and excellent prospects for growth.
- Strong financial conditions.
- Experienced managers.
- Businesses that complement your other tenants.

STEP 5 ▶ *Learn your property*

Even if you use a property manager, you need to know your building, every inch of it. Never forget that you own it and that you are responsible for all that happens there.

Visit the property every month without fail. Check in with your property manager at least that often, but even if she tells you everything's perfect, look for yourself. Until you have a few properties under your belt and have built up a rapport and trust with your property manager, confirm her reports with your own observations. Even after you reach that level of trust, you should still verify, though you can probably get away with visiting less often.

Armed with reports from your initial property inspection, walk the grounds and check the trouble spots. Along the way, you may spot other ones. Based on the reports and your on-site review, set up a renovation plan, fixing problems over time, preferably using cash flow already collected and reserved for that purpose.

The closer you keep watch on your investment, the fewer surprises you'll face and the more effectively you'll deal with those issues.

STEP 6 ▶ *Satisfy your customers*

You purchase property as an investment. But once you own a building and start renting out space, you have, in effect, started a business. And like any business, it will succeed or fail based on the quality and price of the product it provides and the way it treats customers.

When you start thinking of tenants as customers rather than revenue sources, you're on the way to running a good business.

The adage "The customer is always right" overstates the case, as you can't afford to simply bow to every demand. But if your tenants complain or if they request something, always listen. Any business owner can tell you that if you ignore your customers long enough, they'll find another firm to patronize.

To keep your customers satisfied, at some point you'll need to put money back into the property. Respond quickly to complaints about electrical or plumbing issues or leaky roofs. Have your contractors check out the problems; then fix them if needed.

Remember the line for maintenance costs in Pete's cash-flow analysis? Don't be afraid to deploy that cash to keep the building in good condition. And when the building needs major work, something beyond simple maintenance, don't shirk your responsibility. Only a fool buys something of value and fails to protect that value.

Don't kid yourself. When a crucial system in your building stops working, that building starts to lose value. When tenants begin to leave because of the building's problems, you lose near-term cash flow. The building's bad reputation will make it tougher to recruit new tenants, and there goes the long-term cash flow.

Remember those renovation reserves Pete set aside? This is why he did it. When it comes time to repave the parking lot or replace the pipes, you'll understand the reason for those conservative assumptions—and you'll have the cash on hand to pay the contractor.

One more thing before moving on to step 7: Don't go cheap.

This doesn't mean you should throw your money around. But if you hire a cheap exterminator, he may need to visit several times before the ants disappear. Two visits from a bad contractor will probably cost more than one visit from a good one, while your tenants grumble about your lack of action.

Don't just award the job to the lowest bidder. When you select a service professional to address a specific problem, start by soliciting referrals from friends or colleagues. Interview the person before you make a decision, quizzing him on methods, timelines, and a willingness to guarantee his work.

STEP 7 ▶ *Never stop learning*

Like most relationships, owner-tenant interaction becomes easier with time. But only if you learn from your experiences.

Whenever you figure out something that has stumped you in the past, write it down. Over time, you can assemble a large list of these revelations and compile them into an owner's manual of sorts, something customized for your particular property and management style.

You already know that even as you leave specific tasks to the professionals, you must stay engaged, gleaning all the knowledge and techniques you can. To further improve your knowledge base, read books on property management and establish relationships with contacts in the field, such as other property owners as well as managers, lawyers, and accountants you meet while dealing with your own properties.

Real estate isn't a topic you can truly master. However much you know, you still have much to learn. The environment—both economic and geographic—will change, as will the nature of your tenants and their demands. Strategies that worked last year might not work this year, and owners able to adapt stand a better chance of making money consistently over time.

Rights and Responsibilities

Like it or not, as a landlord you must comply with a bevy of rules and regulations. Ignorance of the law is no protection, so take the time to learn what's required.

Yes, you've hired a lawyer. And, of course, your property manager should know the law. But your understanding of the regulations will serve as a check on your manager (so you can recognize when she fails to comply with the law) and give you some clues about when to call that lawyer.

The following paragraphs break down some of the basic requirements you must meet as a landlord:

- **Building safety.** Most states require landlords to comply with the "implied warranty of habitability." This means you must keep your property in a condition fit for tenants to live in, a broad mandate with requirements that vary from state to state. Be aware of the building codes in your municipality and comply with them.

   For the most part, you can meet your responsibilities by promptly fixing problems, particularly those that could result in injury. Keep tabs on your building's heating, plumbing, and electrical systems. Water leaks can cause mold to develop quickly. And if your building doesn't already have carbon-monoxide and smoke detectors, install them immediately.
- **Equal opportunity.** If you reject a tenant, you'd better have a solid, legally protected reason. You can limit your liability by establishing a consistent, written screening policy and providing a copy to any potential tenants. In most jurisdictions you can turn tenants away because of poor credit or references from former landlords; your lawyer can help you draw up a screening policy.
- **Security.** Courts often find landlords legally liable for crimes because of a lack of security. Does this mean you need armed guards roaming the grounds? Probably not. But take steps suitable for the condition of the neighborhood. Consider high-end lock and key systems, alarms, or periodic security sweeps if appropriate. In some cases, you can be held responsible for crimes committed by tenants at your property, such as drug dealing or assaulting other tenants. Your best weapon against this liability is careful tenant screening, use of a security service in high-

TOP FIVE TAX DEDUCTIONS FOR LANDLORDS

1. **Interest.** Interest on a mortgage loan represents the largest expense for many property owners. You can also deduct interest on credit cards or consumer loans if you use that money for the property business.

2. **Depreciation.** If you purchase a building for $500,000, you can't deduct the entire cost. However, you can depreciate that building, deducting a slice of the cost each year. Your accountant can help with this one. When you renovate your property, you can usually depreciate those expenses as well, though in some cases you may simply deduct the costs immediately as repairs.

3. **Repairs.** Most repair expenses qualify as deductions against income.

4. **Wages.** If you pay a property manager or a plumber or a snowplow service, you can deduct the cost as a business expense. This also applies to payments you make to lawyers, accountants, or other professionals who provide services related to the rental business.

5. **Insurance.** In addition to property insurance, you can also deduct any additional liability insurance (many property owners purchase policies related to their landlord activities) or coverage provided to your employees.

Source: Nolo.com

crime neighborhoods, leases that explicitly prohibit illegal conduct, and swift action to evict dangerous tenants.

- **Tax payments.** This is a responsibility not to your tenants, but to yourself and the federal government. Don't listen to anyone who tells you cash flows from investment real estate are not taxable. Depending on your expenses and your accounting system, you may be able to deduct enough to offset the cash flows. However, that's not the same as tax-free cash flows. Ensure that your property manager keeps records of every receipt and expenditure, so your accountant can limit your tax liability as much as possible within the law.

- **No hasty evictions.** Laws regarding evictions and breaking leases vary greatly from state to state. At some point, you'll probably need to evict a tenant, which can become both expensive and unpleasant. Your property manager and lawyer will do most of the work, but familiarize yourself with any applicable laws. Even if you normally take an arm's-length approach to property management, you'll want to keep a close eye on eviction procedures, if only to protect yourself by ensuring that your team is dotting the i's and crossing the t's.

■ **Notification before entry of premises.** Without advance notice (often 24 hours), in most states the owner or property manager can enter a rented space only in an emergency, such as a fire or other serious problem that could damage the building or injure tenants.

The preceding paragraphs focus only on issues that apply throughout the country. Your state has regulations of its own, and many municipalities tack on more. Look up those rules, then keep a copy nearby so you can refer to them when needed.

A Google search for "landlord responsibilities" and the name of your state should point you in the right direction, as you can probably find a newspaper story, property manager, or law firm that has summarized them. If you'd like to read the codes themselves, visit Nolo.com, which lists key statutes from every state.

I firmly believe you have to have a passion for what you do in life in order to succeed. Without passion it can be tough going, and you need to have focus as well. It's important to find out what you like doing, what you're suited for, and then go for it with everything you've got. You have to give 100% or it won't work.

I was initially focused on real estate and becoming a developer. Gradually my interests broadened to include more than real estate. I am essentially a builder, but that can include other things than buildings/skyscrapers. I became a golf course developer because I love the game and that seemed a natural progression for me. I can play golf and survey my courses at the same time.

The Apprentice had a business and educational subtext that also intrigued me and plugged into my acumen as a businessman and a teacher. I believe my diversity evolved once I was established in real estate.

DONALD TRUMP
INTERVIEWED BY *THE WASHINGTON TIMES*

9

ENHANCING VALUE

Owning real estate can pay off in two ways: cash flows and price appreciation. If you buy an occupied building, the cash flows start coming in immediately. However, the increases in property value take longer to manifest.

Remember how the NCREIF Property Index returned 9.4 percent a year from 1978 through 2012? Those returns include increases in the value of the real estate, though the owners don't realize the gains until they sell the property. You want to tap into those gains as well, and you can if you take care of the property. But neither the cash flows nor the price appreciation are guaranteed.

As a real estate owner, you have responsibilities beyond managing the property. Without shrewd stewardship, your building won't rise in value. Remember that commercial property is valued relative to its cash flows. So if you want to add value to your property, focus on boosting those flows.

How do you keep the cash flows rising? Here are seven ways.

1. **Keep up with rents.** Track the movement in rents over time. Whether you use LoopNet.com or another site or a data provider recommended by your agent, make a point of reviewing the numbers in your market every month. By doing this, you can ensure that your rates remain current. Consult with your agent before making any changes, but if rents in your area are trending higher, you might want to boost the rent when your leases expire.
2. **Pay attention to business trends.** Read the business section of your newspaper and watch the local news. Take note of businesses leaving town or moving in.

FIVE TRAITS OF HIGHLY PROFITABLE PROPERTIES

You've already visited the site and analyzed its location. But above and beyond that analysis, you'll improve your odds if you focus on properties with the following characteristics:

- **Youth.** Plenty of people like vintage homes. Vintage office buildings, not so much. Depending on your financial resources, you may not have many options. But if possible, stick to buildings no more than 20 years old, and preferably less than 10 years. Yes, buildings can remain viable for decades. However, repair and maintenance expenses tend to increase as buildings age. Give precedence to newer properties or those that have recently undergone a comprehensive remodeling.

- **Technology.** Not all buildings offer the same amenities, nor should they. Property without the latest communications infrastructure may already have a rent structure and selling price that reflects the lack. However, investors should always look forward. So ask yourself, "Will I still be able to attract even midlevel tenants 10 years from now if I don't upgrade the building's technology?" If the answer is no, either buy something with more amenities or build the upgrade costs into your cash-flow model.

- **Brick or stone.** Wooden buildings, in addition to being susceptible to fire, cost more to operate. Wood wears out faster than masonry, and you'll need to paint it more often. And don't forget about woodpeckers, termites, and squirrels in search of a warm place to spend the winter.

- **Inefficient use.** If the current owner charges rents lower than the market can bear or doesn't make the best use of the space, you can probably add value to the property by boosting the cash flow after you take over. In addition, the current owner's lower cash flows may cause him to value the building below your target price.

- **Peaked roof.** Flat roofs cost more in the long run. Rain pools and snow gathers— and no matter how well you maintain the roof, standing water will eventually make it into the building.

Follow the labor market nationally, and locally if the municipal government tracks employment data. The more you understand about business conditions, the easier you'll find it to respond to changes in the attitude and behavior of your tenants and to decide whether or not to raise rents.

3. **Conduct cost surveys.** At least once a year, call other service providers to see if you're getting the best deal. You may not want to switch providers just to save a small amount of money, but if you can arrange for landscaping services, trash pickup, security, or maintenance at lower costs than you're currently paying, you owe it to yourself to consider a change. If you want to stay with an existing pro-

vider despite his higher costs because he either provides superior services or has developed a valuable relationship with you, then do so. But when you know about alternatives to your current situation, you enjoy greater flexibility to act when the time is right.

4. **Learn from your tenants.** Renters will complain. It's what they do. Either you or your property manager will deal with the issues, and some beefs have more merit than others. But even if you think the renter is talking through her hat, record the complaint politely and keep a record. Every two or three months, look at the complaints and see if you can spot trends. If you hear a half dozen complaints about ants in June when only one person brought the topic up in May, it's probably time to call the exterminator.

   Property owners can get too caught up in responding to complaints in real time to see the bigger picture. So step back and look for it periodically. This perspective will help you deal with acute problems that require one-time remediation as well as chronic problems that may warrant a renovation or an upgrade project. Either way, the sooner you spot the signs, the earlier you can begin setting money aside.

5. **Follow up on financing.** Interest rates change, and so do lending policies. Refinancing a loan costs money up front, but sometimes it makes sense if you can substantially reduce your borrowing costs.

6. **Update your property.** A real estate investor could easily spend 100 percent of his yearly cash flows and more on renovations; no building will ever be perfect. But way too many investors deploy almost no money toward renovations, a good recipe for eroding the building's value over time. Don't be afraid to commit the money you've set aside for renovations, if those renovations will make the building more appealing to new tenants. When possible, focus on small, cost-effective projects. Give particular attention to the following:

   - **The exterior.** Peeling paint, ragged bushes, and cracked pavement provide an aura of neglect and unprofessionalism. New siding will cost quite a bit up front but can provide a building with a fresh façade for years.
   - **Signage.** If your building has a sign announcing either its name or the identity of the tenants, keep that valuable marketing tool looking bright and crisp. Nothing detracts from the look of a property like a sign with lights that don't work or a huge tree obscuring the words.
   - **The roof.** Leaky roofs can cause massive damage in minutes, costing you money and angering your tenants. Never ignore complaints about leaks, and check the integrity of your roof at least once a year.
   - **Subpar communications.** Even small tenants expect high-volume computer and telecom systems. Office-building owners in particular should understand that if you can't satisfy a modern business's communications needs, you'll have trouble filling vacant space.

- **Carpeting.** Everyone notices carpet. Keep it clean, and replace it before it starts to look ratty.
7. **Focus on business-friendly areas.** This point requires action before you buy. But if you purchase property in a city with a planning or zoning board that allows a lot of new construction, you'll probably encounter fewer hassles when it's time to expand or renovate your building.

Growing Your Empire

You may have noticed that the preceding list didn't include adding on to the existing property. That issue requires its own section, because it goes beyond simply boosting cash flows.

Of course, because you're no fool, you'll consider investing more money in real estate only if you meet the following conditions:

- Your existing building operates smoothly, generating sufficient cash flow to provide a solid return in excess of expenses.
- You've become comfortable with the process of purchasing and owning real estate.
- Your target market enjoys favorable trends—job growth, rising rental rates, economic expansion, and so on.
- You can afford to pay at least a significant portion of any new mortgage loan out of cash flows you already receive, and you've set aside sufficient cash for a robust down payment. Once you've taken on a commercial loan, your ratio of debt to income may cause lenders to hesitate. A large up-front payment and income generous enough to cover another interest payment will make you more appealing to lenders.
- Owning more real estate makes sense, given the condition of your investment portfolio. For instance, if one building accounts for 40 percent of your net worth, you might be better served sinking your cash into traditional investments.

Expanding your real estate holdings will increase the amount of time you spend analyzing and managing them. Even if you employ a property manager, once you acquire a certain number of buildings, you'll become a full-time real estate investor.

However, buying the second property will not be quite as taxing as the first purchase. For one thing, you've already assembled your team. You may have to pay your lawyer and accountant more because you ask more of them. But once you've found competent professionals you can trust, they should be able to handle more than one property for you. Plus, by this point you've presumably assembled a stable of contacts in the industry.

If you do opt to buy more property, don't forget the basics. Put the same care into finding and analyzing your second building that you did with your first. It's human nature to revel in our successes and attribute much of it to our own stupendous ability—a dangerous weakness.

Most professional athletes excel at every level of competition starting in their earliest years. Natural talent has provided them with an edge over everyone else, whether they worked hard or not. However, once they reach the professional level, athletes learn that everyone is supremely talented.

Any sports fan can dredge up a tale of athletes who, despite awesome physical skills, never realize their full potential. Often this lack of achievement stems from laziness. Or, more specifically, a belief that they can achieve success at the highest level without working any harder than they did in high school. They might have put forth the effort during the early days of their professional careers. But once the money starts rolling in, plenty of athletes slack off.

Don't fall into that trap, no matter how well your first building has performed. The Apostle Paul said it best in 1 Corinthians, chapter 10: "Wherefore let him that thinketh he standeth take heed lest he fall."

Be warned. Don't let up on the quality control and attention to detail that drove your early success, and don't ramp up the risk.

Other Ways to Invest

Concerned about overleveraging your finances or overcommitting your time? If so, you can invest in real estate without the hassles of purchasing physical property.

By now you know that real estate investors can make money with office, industrial, retail, and residential property. While the businesses aren't exactly simple, most people understand the gist of how they operate, and all four use a fairly similar business model:

- Find tenants to lease space.
- Collect rent.
- Maintain the property and address tenant concerns.

This book focuses on direct ownership of rental property, an established method of both generating cash and building wealth. However, some types of real estate don't operate under the same business model, requiring a different type of commitment from investors. Other real estate investments revolve around the old faithful own-and-operate model but allow the investor to delegate those responsibilities to someone else.

Options for direct ownership include the following:

- **Farmland or timberland.** As is the case with hotels, owning and operating farms or logging operations requires a focus not on finding tenants, but on the extraction of commodities. If you wish to become a farmer or operate a lumber company, go for it. However, these properties won't appeal to the typical investor who'd purchase an office building.

- **Rehab.** Buying real estate to fix up and resell requires a different focus than managing property for rental. For the most part, this business model works only if you can act fast, and the profit margins make sense only if you can do the work for a bargain price.
- **Vacant land.** You may have heard of someone who purchased a field next to a country road for $50,000 and then sold it to a developer for $1 million a decade later, after the city grew into the area. While these deals do happen, few yield such an impressive profit. And you don't hear about all the years paying property taxes without collecting any revenue or the worries that developers would instead focus on the other side of town.

  Successful land speculation requires a knowledge of economic-development and construction trends, a network of industry and government contacts, and a healthy dollop of luck. For the most part, unless you possess the resources to cover the taxes on the land and eventually develop it yourself if no buyer materializes, land speculation rarely makes sense.
- **Rental houses.** Think of this investment as "multifamily light." You'll pay more for the property relative to the income it generates, but owning a single unit requires less work. And if you decide to sell the property, a house should move more easily. However, if you wish to make a business of real estate, multifamily offers the opportunity for greater cash flow relative to the amount of time needed to manage the property. For instance, you might be able to buy a six-flat building that generates rents similar to what you could collect from four houses. But you have only one physical property to maintain, and you can interact with all of your tenants at the same place.

Investors can also get into real estate indirectly, without owning the properties themselves. Some brokerages or investment firms manage private real estate funds. Levels of profit, risk, expense, and disclosure vary greatly, and most investors will find such funds difficult to assess. Instead, go with something publicly traded.

Real estate investment trusts (REITs) trade on public exchanges like stocks, providing greater liquidity than direct investments in property. Investors buy trust units that reflect a small ownership interest in the company, and thus the property it controls.

According to the National Association of Real Estate Investment Trusts (NAREIT), 172 REITs traded at the end of 2012, with a total stock-market value of more than $600 billion. A decade earlier, all the REITs had a combined market value of $162 billion. Price appreciation of commercial property can't account for all those gains. The increase in market value also reflects greater investor interest in REITs and aggressive property acquisition.

REITs come in a variety of flavors. Some focus on specific types of property, while others own diversified holdings. Mortgage REITs don't own property, instead holding packages of mortgage loans.

In order to qualify as a REIT, a company must keep at least 75 percent of its assets in real estate–related investments, and those assets must generate at least 75 percent of company profits. To top it off, REITs must distribute at least 90 percent of their income to shareholders, which means these investments can offer yields well above those of the average stock.

If REITs meet the income and distribution rules, they usually pay no corporate income tax, which helps fund those generous dividends. Historically, REITs have delivered solid returns. The NAREIT U.S. Real Estate Index, a broad basket of stocks designed to track the REIT industry, notched a total return of 554 percent from 1994 through 2013, versus 483 percent for the S&P 500 Index of large-company stocks. Total returns assume all cash flows are reinvested in the index.

Going forward, investors shouldn't count on REITs to continue to outperform the broad stock market. But investors who seek real estate exposure without the hassle of owning the property itself may find REITs of interest.

Note that while REITs have appeal, they don't provide the intangible benefits of owning real property. Nor do they allow you to invest locally or to develop a deep understanding of the property that interests you. And if you look at real estate as a diversification tool, REITs don't help as much as direct ownership of property. In recent years, REITs' returns have provided less diversification relative to stocks than they once did. REITs may provide real estate exposure, but direct ownership of rental property still looks and feels like a different type of investment.

Protecting Your Investment

One of the best ways to improve the value of your investment is to preserve what you already have.

In the previous pages you learned strategies for boosting cash flows over time. But no matter how much effort you put into growing the business, it will crumble without a firm foundation. With that in mind, here are five steps to avoid the type of disaster that will erode your cash flows from within.

STEP 1 ▶ *Maintain the property*

Yes, this isn't the first time you've read such advice. But some truths warrant repetition.

When you first analyze a potential property's cash flows, you'll probably feel the urge to either ignore maintenance expenses ("I'll start taking care of the property next year, after I make a little money,") or underestimate them ("I can't have the same kind of bad luck the former owner did").

REITS OUTPERFORM BROAD STOCK INDEX

Since the start of 1994, the NAREIT U.S. Real Estate Index has returned 554%, assuming dividends were reinvested in the index, versus a 483% return for the S&P 500 Index of large-company stocks. This chart shows the cumulative total return since start of 1994.

Date	NAREIT U.S. Real Estate Index	S&P 500 Index	Date	NAREIT U.S. Real Estate Index	S&P 500 Index
Dec 2013	554%	483%	Sep 2010	357%	236%
Nov 2013	549%	469%	Aug 2010	337%	208%
Oct 2013	578%	452%	Jul 2010	343%	223%
Sep 2013	552%	428%	Jun 2010	307%	202%
Aug 2013	530%	412%	May 2010	326%	218%
Jul 2013	571%	427%	Apr 2010	350%	246%
Jun 2013	568%	401%	Mar 2010	322%	241%
May 2013	583%	408%	Feb 2010	286%	221%
Apr 2013	631%	397%	Jan 2010	267%	212%
Mar 2013	591%	387%	Dec 2009	285%	223%
Feb 2013	569%	370%	Nov 2009	262%	217%
Jan 2013	561%	363%	Oct 2009	239%	199%
Dec 2012	534%	340%	Sep 2009	256%	205%
Nov 2012	514%	337%	Aug 2009	235%	194%
Oct 2012	518%	334%	Jul 2009	198%	184%
Sep 2012	520%	342%	Jun 2009	171%	164%
Aug 2012	526%	331%	May 2009	178%	163%
Jul 2012	523%	322%	Apr 2009	172%	149%
Jun 2012	509%	316%	Mar 2009	112%	128%
May 2012	475%	299%	Feb 2009	103%	109%
Apr 2012	499%	325%	Jan 2009	152%	134%
Mar 2012	482%	328%	Dec 2008	202%	156%
Feb 2012	458%	314%	Nov 2008	161%	153%
Jan 2012	462%	297%	Oct 2008	232%	172%
Dec 2011	427%	280%	Sep 2008	376%	227%
Nov 2011	404%	276%	Aug 2008	378%	259%
Oct 2011	423%	277%	Jul 2008	369%	254%
Sep 2011	361%	240%	Jun 2008	356%	257%
Aug 2011	415%	265%	May 2008	414%	290%
Jul 2011	443%	286%	Apr 2008	410%	285%
Jun 2011	440%	294%	Mar 2008	380%	267%
May 2011	455%	301%	Feb 2008	363%	269%
Apr 2011	451%	306%	Jan 2008	381%	281%
Mar 2011	425%	294%	Dec 2007	382%	306%
Feb 2011	432%	294%	Nov 2007	405%	308%
Jan 2011	410%	281%	Oct 2007	452%	326%
Dec 2010	392%	272%	Sep 2007	448%	320%
Nov 2010	370%	249%	Aug 2007	426%	305%
Oct 2010	377%	249%	Jul 2007	398%	299%

REITS OUTPERFORM BROAD STOCK INDEX

Date	NAREIT U.S. Real Estate Index	S&P 500 Index	Date	NAREIT U.S. Real Estate Index	S&P 500 Index
Jun 2007	446%	311%	Nov 2003	199%	171%
May 2007	501%	318%	Oct 2003	186%	169%
Apr 2007	500%	304%	Sep 2003	180%	155%
Mar 2007	499%	287%	Aug 2003	172%	157%
Feb 2007	515%	283%	Jul 2003	171%	152%
Jan 2007	533%	290%	Jun 2003	157%	148%
Dec 2006	487%	285%	May 2003	151%	145%
Nov 2006	494%	279%	Apr 2003	136%	133%
Oct 2006	469%	272%	Mar 2003	125%	115%
Sep 2006	435%	260%	Feb 2003	121%	113%
Aug 2006	425%	251%	Jan 2003	117%	116%
Jul 2006	408%	243%	Dec 2002	124%	122%
Jun 2006	393%	241%	Nov 2002	121%	136%
May 2006	369%	241%	Oct 2002	111%	123%
Apr 2006	383%	251%	Sep 2002	122%	105%
Mar 2006	398%	246%	Aug 2002	131%	130%
Feb 2006	374%	242%	Jul 2002	131%	128%
Jan 2006	368%	241%	Jun 2002	143%	147%
Dec 2005	337%	232%	May 2002	136%	166%
Nov 2005	338%	232%	Apr 2002	133%	168%
Oct 2005	320%	220%	Mar 2002	130%	186%
Sep 2005	332%	225%	Feb 2002	117%	175%
Aug 2005	332%	223%	Jan 2002	113%	181%
Jul 2005	351%	226%	Dec 2001	112%	185%
Jun 2005	323%	214%	Nov 2001	107%	182%
May 2005	304%	214%	Oct 2001	96%	162%
Apr 2005	290%	204%	Sep 2001	102%	157%
Mar 2005	273%	210%	Aug 2001	110%	180%
Feb 2005	280%	215%	Jul 2001	103%	199%
Jan 2005	272%	209%	Jun 2001	107%	202%
Dec 2004	304%	217%	May 2001	96%	209%
Nov 2004	285%	206%	Apr 2001	91%	207%
Oct 2004	268%	194%	Mar 2001	86%	185%
Sep 2004	252%	190%	Feb 2001	84%	204%
Aug 2004	251%	187%	Jan 2001	87%	235%
Jul 2004	226%	186%	Dec 2000	84%	223%
Jun 2004	225%	195%	Nov 2000	72%	222%
May 2004	216%	190%	Oct 2000	70%	249%
Apr 2004	195%	186%	Sep 2000	78%	251%
Mar 2004	248%	190%	Aug 2000	72%	270%
Feb 2004	230%	195%	Jul 2000	79%	249%
Jan 2004	223%	191%	Jun 2000	65%	254%
Dec 2003	209%	186%	May 2000	61%	246%

(continued)

REITS OUTPERFORM BROAD STOCK INDEX

(continued from previous page)

Date	NAREIT U.S. Real Estate Index	S&P 500 Index	Date	NAREIT U.S. Real Estate Index	S&P 500 Index
Apr 2000	59%	253%	Jan 1997	64%	82%
Mar 2000	49%	264%	Dec 1996	62%	71%
Feb 2000	45%	231%	Nov 1996	47%	75%
Jan 2000	47%	238%	Oct 1996	41%	63%
Dec 1999	46%	256%	Sep 1996	36%	58%
Nov 1999	42%	236%	Aug 1996	34%	50%
Oct 1999	45%	229%	Jul 1996	29%	47%
Sep 1999	49%	210%	Jun 1996	28%	53%
Aug 1999	54%	218%	May 1996	26%	53%
Jul 1999	58%	220%	Apr 1996	23%	49%
Jun 1999	64%	230%	Mar 1996	22%	47%
May 1999	66%	213%	Feb 1996	22%	45%
Apr 1999	63%	220%	Jan 1996	22%	44%
Mar 1999	48%	208%	Dec 1995	19%	39%
Feb 1999	49%	197%	Nov 1995	13%	37%
Jan 1999	53%	206%	Oct 1995	12%	31%
Dec 1998	56%	194%	Sep 1995	14%	31%
Nov 1998	61%	178%	Aug 1995	12%	26%
Oct 1998	58%	162%	Jul 1995	10%	26%
Sep 1998	63%	142%	Jun 1995	9%	22%
Aug 1998	53%	128%	May 1995	7%	19%
Jul 1998	71%	166%	Apr 1995	2%	15%
Jun 1998	83%	169%	Mar 1995	2%	11%
May 1998	84%	158%	Feb 1995	3%	8%
Apr 1998	85%	163%	Jan 1995	−1%	4%
Mar 1998	91%	160%	Dec 1994	1%	1%
Feb 1998	88%	148%	Nov 1994	−5%	0%
Jan 1998	92%	131%	Oct 1994	−2%	4%
Dec 1997	92%	128%	Sep 1994	2%	1%
Nov 1997	89%	125%	Aug 1994	4%	4%
Oct 1997	86%	115%	Jul 1994	3%	0%
Sep 1997	90%	122%	Jun 1994	4%	−3%
Aug 1997	76%	111%	May 1994	6%	−1%
Jul 1997	77%	123%	Apr 1994	4%	−2%
Jun 1997	72%	107%	Mar 1994	2%	−4%
May 1997	64%	98%	Feb 1994	7%	1%
Apr 1997	59%	86%	Jan 1994	3%	3%
Mar 1997	62%	76%	Dec 1993	0%	0%
Feb 1997	64%	83%			

Sources: NAREIT, Standard & Poor's

What you write off as "bad luck" may simply reflect a steady stream of needed maintenance costs that you'll incur as well. And even if the numbers you dismiss turn out to be just a run of poor luck, you could certainly encounter the same problems.

Action: Consider all the potential maintenance expenses, consulting your agent, property manager, and any repair professionals you intend to hire. Then pay attention to the spending records of the former owner. Look at what was spent last year, over the last 3 years, and over the last 10 years if you can get those numbers. Gauge the trends; if maintenance expenses have risen over time, assume they will continue to do so. If you don't see a trend, set your annual budget based on the long-run average.

If the property is in good repair, start by setting aside 15 percent to 20 percent more than the last owner spent. If the building is in poor repair, be prepared to double the spending to spruce the place up.

STEP 2 ▶ *Insure against loss*

Everybody should pay for liability insurance, even people who don't own property. Relative to the value of the property—and to the size of the lawsuits possible if some-body sprints across your lawn and breaks his leg tripping over a tree trunk, or slips and falls in your bathroom—it tends to cost very little. If you own property, the num-ber of people who might sue skyrockets, as do their possible reasons for litigation and the amounts they'll expect to collect.

If you're one of those people who likes to dodge the rules or live dangerously, like eschewing collision coverage because you're too good a driver to damage your car or not telling your life-insurance provider that you skydive every weekend, set those tendencies aside. Tell the insurance company what you do and what kind of coverage you expect. Then pay the premium for liability insurance and be glad you're covered.

However, you may be able to save some money on the property-damage side if you opt to insure the building for enough money to pay off the loan and provide a down payment on another building, rather than for replacement cost. Unless you'd opt to rebuild after a disaster, which may cost far more than purchasing a new build-ing, you need not buy replacement coverage. Of course, if you own a newer building that sells for something close to its replacement cost, you might as well purchase full coverage.

Action: Buy insurance specifically designed for property owners. It should provide high-dollar (think seven or eight figures) liability coverage and broad-based reim-bursement for damages to the building.

STEP 3 ▶ *Establish legal protections*

Never forget that owning real estate is like operating a business. Anyone can sue the company, but if you take the proper precautions, they shouldn't be able to get at your personal assets. You have two primary options:

- *A corporation*: This entity provides protection against most liability, though the level of protection varies from state to state. However, if your own negligence causes someone else to become injured or lose something of value, all bets are off.
- *A limited liability company (LLC)*: LLCs take a step beyond the typical corporation, combining the corporate structure with that of a partnership or sole proprietorship. This arrangement prevents members (owners of an LLC are called members) from being held personally liable for the company's debts. LLCs offer more protection than a typical corporation but require extra paperwork. For instance, they must be dissolved if one of the members dies or declares bankruptcy. LLCs also offer tax benefits; your accountant can fill you in.

Action: Because LLCs offer more protection, most real estate investors should opt for that corporate structure. However, rules vary from state to state. Talk to your lawyer about preparing the proper documents and to learn the limits of the LLC's protection.

STEP 4 ▶ *Share the financial burden*

For many individuals, buying real estate is out of reach, even using leverage. In some cases, you may wish to go in with one or more partners. Perhaps you seek to raise more capital for the purchase. Perhaps you wish to bring in a seasoned real estate pro while you provide the funds. Or perhaps you simply want to collaborate with a friend or relative.

Most individual investors will have trouble qualifying for a commercial mortgage loan their first time around. Approaching the banker with the backing of partners may make a difference, as a lender should look favorably on granting a loan to a group of people with more assets and/or established expertise in the field.

You may be tempted to join forces with friends or relatives, but understand that pooling money will test the strength of relationships, because people often behave differently when cash is on the line. No matter how well you and your partners get along right now, always account for the possibility that you will at some point disagree on how to manage the investment.

Action: If you do set up a partnership, make sure it provides ways to address illegal conduct by one of the partners and sort out differences of opinion. As is the case with most business entities, states establish their own laws, so consult both your lawyer and your accountant.

STEP 5 ▶ *Pay attention*

It sounds simple, but humans get stuck in ruts, and it becomes easy to assume that an investment doing well now will continue to perform just as strongly in the future. However, change is the only constant. Own property for long enough, and the environment will shift, forcing you to shift with it.

Read all you can on business and legal trends, particularly as they relate to real estate. Remember all those boring newspaper stories about zoning board meetings? The ones you skipped over while turning to the sports page? Start reading them, because any change in zoning, permitting, property taxes, or a host of other subjects could affect how your property operates and thus affect your investment.

Action: Keep up with political developments at the local level. Some candidates are friendlier to property owners than others, and you should understand the thinking of the people who govern your city.

Don't feel you must become a political activist. Most business owners can do just fine no matter who is in charge—as long as they keep up with changes that affect their companies. Don't be that guy who puts off a major expansion project for years, only to discover that by the time he's ready to go, the city has decided to restrict new construction in his neighborhood. Such policy changes rarely happen overnight, and property owners who pay attention have a better chance of spotting the warning signs.

The End Game

At this point, you know most of what you need to succeed in commercial real estate. You've learned how the rental property market works, how to find and analyze buildings, and what to do with them after you buy. You've realized the power of assembling a good team and letting the experts do their work. And you're ready to take steps to increase the value of your property over time.

But still, you need a little bit more. Something you can't glean from this book or any other book. There is truly no substitute for experience. Take the lessons you've already learned and then add to them as you encounter your unique roadblocks. Because you *will* run into troubles—some this book warned about, as well as others specific to the property you chose to acquire.

When the crisis comes and your cash flows go negative, don't follow in the footsteps of the flood of foolish investors who jump to one of two conclusions:

1. *Real estate isn't the investment I had hoped for. All those people who said you can make money with real estate were blowing smoke.*

Admittedly, you won't get any guarantees with real estate. Yes, you can lose money. And at some point, you probably will, at least temporarily.

This is where taking a long-term view becomes important. If you purchased property for the right reason and your cash flows suffer because of storms you can't control, do your best to cope with those forces and be patient. Revisit your finances and your property operations, consulting with your experts to spot areas for improvement. And have confidence that storms do eventually blow themselves out.

2. *I'm an idiot and I can't do this. I should just sell this dump for pennies on the dollar and stick to savings accounts.*

Truthfully, at times you may be an idiot. Most people don the dunce cap from time to time, particularly when they try new things. But temporary failure shouldn't drive you to a permanent decision to quit.

Keep reading and learning and studying. You'll get better. With time and effort, you can develop a deeper understanding of the real estate market and how the industry operates.

Plenty of tycoons started out with nothing but a few thousand square feet, a big mortgage, and a willingness to work. That formula can still pay off.

Sample Letter of Intent

LETTER OF INTENT TO PURCHASE REAL ESTATE

The purpose of this letter is to set for the some of the basic terms and conditions of the proposed purchase by the undersigned (the "Buyer") of certain real estate owned by you (the "Seller"). The terms set forth in this Letter will not become binding until a more detailed "Purchase Agreement" is negotiated and signed by the parties, as contemplated below by the section of this Letter entitled "Non-Binding."

1. PROPERTY ADDRESS: The property proposed to be sold is located at:

_____

2. PRICE: The proposed purchase price is $_____, of which $_____ would be deposited in Escrow, upon acceptance of a binding Purchase Agreement. Buyer would pay the balance to Seller at closing.

3. POSSESSION: Possession would be given on _____, or sooner by mutual agreement. Settlement would be made at the closing, immediately prior to possession.

4. INSPECTION: After the final acceptance of a binding Purchase Agreement, Buyer may have the Real Estate inspected by a person of Buyer's choice to determine if there are any structural, mechanical, plumbing or electrical deficiencies, structural pest damage or infestation, any unsafe conditions or other damage, including the presence of radon gas, any lead-based paint hazards, and inspections for other conditions that are customary to the locality and/or that are required by law.

5. FINANCING:

6. CLOSING COSTS: Traditional distribution of closing costs.

7. STANDARD PROVISIONS: The Purchase Agreement will include the standard provisions that are customary to the locality and/or that are required by law.

8. ADDITIONAL PROVISIONS: _____
_____
_____

9. STAND STILL: Seller shall not initiate or carry on negotiations for the sale of the Real Estate with any party other than Buyer unless either (1) Buyer and Seller fail to enter into a binding Purchase Agreement by 72 HOURS from the time of

acceptance of this agreement, or (2) Buyer and Seller agree in writing to abandon this Letter of Intent.

10. NON-BINDING. This letter of Intent does not and is not intended to contractually bind the parties, and is only an expression of the basic conditions to be incorporated into a binding Purchasing Agreement. This Letter does not require either party to negotiate in good faith or to proceed to the completion of a binding Purchase Agreement. The parties shall not be contractually bound unless and until they enter into a formal, written Purchase Agreement, which must be in form and content satisfactory to each party and to each party's legal counsel, in their sole discretion.

Neither party may rely on this Letter as creating any legal obligation of any kind. Notwithstanding the provisions of this paragraph to the contrary, Seller and Buyer agree that the above paragraph entitled "Stand Still" shall be binding, regardless of whether a binding Purchase Agreement is entered into the parties.

If you would like to discuss a sale of Real Estate with the undersigned on these general terms, please sign and return a copy of this Letter of Intent to the undersigned at your earliest convenience.

Very truly yours,

The above Letter reflects our mutual understanding and sets forth the basis for proceedings tonegotiate a Purchase Agreement as outlined above.

SELLER: BUYER:

_____   _____

_____   _____

DATE OF ACCEPTANCE:

_____

Sample Purchase and Sale Agreement

This sample agreement is customized for New York state, and is intended to be used as a reference only.

Contract of Sale made as of _____

between _____,

Address: _____,

Social Security Number/ Fed. I.D. No(s): _____, hereinafter called **"Seller"** and _____,

Address: _____,

Social Security Number/Fed. I.D. No(s): _____, hereinafter called **"Purchaser"**.

The parties hereby agree as follows:

1. Premises.

Seller shall sell and convey and Purchaser shall purchase the property, together with all buildings and improvements thereon (collectively the **"Premises"**), more fully described on a separate page marked "Schedule A", annexed hereto and made a part hereof and also known as: _____

Street Address: _____.

Tax Map Designation: _____.

Together with Seller's ownership and rights, if any, to land lying in the bed of any street or highway, opened or proposed, adjoining the Premises to the center line thereof, including any right of Seller to any unpaid award by reason of any taking by condemnation and/or for any damage to the Premises by reason of change of grade of any street or highway. Seller shall deliver at no additional cost to Purchaser, at Closing (as hereinafter defined), or thereafter, on demand, any documents that Purchaser may reasonably require for the conveyance of such title and the assignment and collection of such award or damages.

2. Personal Property.

This sale also includes all fixtures and articles of personal property now attached or appurtenant to the Premises, unless specifically excluded below. Seller represents and warrants that at Closing they will be paid for and owned by Seller, free and clear of all liens and encumbrances, except any existing mortgage to which this sale may be subject. They include, but are not limited to, plumbing, heating, lighting and cooking fixtures, chandeliers, bathroom and kitchen cabinets and counters, mantels, door mirrors, switch plates and door hardware, venetian blinds, window treatments, shades, screens, awnings, storm windows, storm doors, window boxes, mail box, TV aerials, weather vane, flagpole, pumps, shrubbery, fencing, outdoor statuary, tool shed, dishwasher, washing machine, clothes dryer, garbage disposal unit, range, oven, built-in microwave oven, refrigerator, freezer, air conditioning equipment and installations, wall to wall carpeting and built ins not excluded below (*strike out inapplicable items*).

Excluded from this sale are furniture and household furnishings and _____ _____ .

3. Purchase Price. The purchase price is _____ ($_____), payable as follows:

(a) on the signing of this contract, by Purchaser's good check payable to the Escrowee (as hereinafter defined), subject to collection, the receipt of which is hereby acknowledged, to be held in escrow pursuant to paragraph 6 of this contract (the **"Downpayment"**): $_____.

(b) by allowance for the principal amount unpaid on the existing mortgage on the date hereof, payment of which Purchaser shall assume by joinder in the deed: $_____.

(c) by a purchase money note and mortgage from Purchaser to Seller: $_____.

(d) balance at Closing in accordance with paragraph 7: $_____.

4. Existing Mortgage. (*Delete if inapplicable*) If this sale is subject to an existing mortgage as indicated in paragraph 3(b) above:

(a) The Premises shall be conveyed subject to the continuing lien of the existing mortgage, which is presently payable, with interest at the rate of _____ percent per annum, in monthly installments of $_____ which include principal, interest an escrow amounts, if any, and with any balance of principal being due and payable on _____.

(b) To the extent that any required payments are made on the existing mortgage between the date hereof and Closing which reduce the unpaid principal amount thereof below the amount shown in paragraph 3(b), then the balance of the price payable at Closing under paragraph 3(d) shall be increased by the amount of the payments of principal. Seller represents and warrants that the amount shown in paragraph 3(b) is substantially correct and agrees that only payments required by the existing mortgage will be made between the date hereof and Closing.

(c) If there is a mortgagee escrow account, Seller shall assign it to Purchaser, if it can be assigned, and in that case Purchaser shall pay the amount in the escrow account to Seller at Closing.

(d) Seller shall deliver to Purchaser at Closing a certificate dated not more than _____ days before Closing signed by the holder of the existing mortgage, in form for recording, certifying the amount of the unpaid principal, the date to which interest has been paid and the amounts, if any, claimed to be unpaid for principal and interest, itemizing the same. Seller shall pay the fees for recording such certificate. If the holder of the existing mortgage is a bank or other institution as defined in Section 274 a of the Real Property Law it may, instead of the certificate, furnish a letter signed by a duly authorized officer, employee or agent, dated not more than 30 days before Closing, containing the same information.

(e) Seller represents and warrants that (i) Seller has delivered to Purchaser true and complete copies of the existing mortgage, the note secured thereby and any extensions and modifications thereof, (ii) the existing mortgage is not now, and at the time of Closing will not be, in default, and (iii) the existing mortgage does not contain any provision that permits the holder of the mortgage to require its immediate payment in full or to change any other term thereof by reason of the sale or conveyance of the Premises.

5. Purchase Money Mortgage. (*Delete if inapplicable*) If there is to be a purchase money mortgage as indicated in paragraph 3(c) above:

(a) The purchase money note and mortgage shall be drawn by the attorney for Seller in the form attached or, if not, in the standard form adopted by the New York State Land Title Association. Purchaser shall pay at Closing the mortgage recording tax, recording fees and the attorney's fees in the amount of $_____ for its preparation.

(b) The purchase money note and mortgage shall also provide that it is subject and subordinate to the lien of the existing mortgage and any extensions, modifications, replacements or consolidations of the existing mortgage, provided that (i) the interest rate thereof shall not be greater than Interest percent per annum and the total debt service thereunder shall not be greater than $_____ per annum, and (ii) if the principal amount thereof shall exceed the amount of principal owing and unpaid on the existing mortgage at the time of placing such new mortgage or consolidated mortgage, the excess be paid to the holder of such purchase money mortgage in reduction of the principal thereof. The purchase money mortgage shall also provide that such payment to the holder thereof shall not alter or affect the regular installments, if any, of principal payable thereunder and that the holder thereof will, on demand and without charge therefore, execute, acknowledge and deliver any agreement or agreements further to effectuate such subordination.

6. Downpayment in Escrow.

(a) Seller's attorney (**"Escrowee"**) shall hold the Downpayment in escrow in a seg-
regated bank account at _____, address: _____,
until Closing or sooner termination of this contract and shall pay over or apply
the Downpayment in accordance with the terms of this paragraph. Escrowee
shall hold the Downpayment in a(n) _____ bearing account for
the benefit of the parties. If interest is held for the benefit of the parties, it shall be
paid to the party entitled to the Downpayment and the party receiving the interest shall pay any income taxes thereon. If interest is not held for the benefit of
the parties, the Downpayment shall be placed in an IOLA account or as otherwise
permitted or required by law. The Social Security or Federal Identification numbers of the parties shall be furnished to Escrowee upon request. At Closing, the
Downpayment shall be paid by Escrowee to Seller. If for any reason Closing does
not occur and either party gives Notice (as defined in paragraph 25) to Escrowee
demanding payment of the Downpayment, Escrowee shall give prompt Notice to
the other party of such demand. If Escrowee does not receive Notice of objection
from such other party to the proposed payment within _____ business
days after the giving of such Notice, Escrowee is hereby authorized and directed
to make such payment. If Escrowee does receive such Notice of objection within
such 10 day period or if for any other reason Escrowee in good faith shall elect not
to make such payment, Escrowee shall continue to hold such amount until otherwise directed by Notice from the parties to this contract or a final, nonappealable
judgment, order or decree of a court. However, Escrowee shall have the right at
any time to deposit the Downpayment and the interest thereon with the clerk of
a court in the county in which the Premises are located and shall give Notice of
such deposit to Seller and Purchaser. Upon such deposit or other disbursement
in accordance with the terms of this paragraph, Escrowee shall be relieved and
discharged of all further obligations and responsibilities hereunder.

(b) The parties acknowledge that Escrowee is acting solely as a stakeholder at their
request and for their convenience and that Escrowee shall not be liable to either
party for any act or omission on its part unless taken or suffered in bad faith or
in willful disregard of this contract or involving gross negligence on the part of
Escrowee. Seller and Purchaser jointly and severally (with right of contribu-
tion) agree to defend (by attorneys selected by Escrowee), indemnify and hold
Escrowee harmless from and against all costs, claims and expenses (including
reasonable attorneys' fees) incurred in connection with the performance of
Escrowee's duties hereunder, except with respect to actions or omissions taken or
suffered by Escrowee in bad faith or in willful disregard of this contract or involving gross negligence on the part of Escrowee.

(c) Escrowee may act or refrain from acting in respect of any matter referred to herein in full reliance upon and with the advice of counsel which may be selected by it (including any member of its firm) and shall be fully protected in so acting or refraining from action upon the advice of such counsel.

(d) Escrowee acknowledges receipt of the Downpayment by check subject to collection and Escrowee's agreement to the provisions of this paragraph by signing in the place indicated on the signature page of this contract.

(e) Escrowee or any member of its firm shall be permitted to act as counsel for Seller in any dispute as to the disbursement of the Downpayment or any other dispute between the parties whether or not Escrowee is in possession of the Downpayment and continues to act as Escrowee.

(f) The party whose attorney is Escrowee shall be liable for loss of the Downpayment.

7. Acceptable Funds. All money payable under this contract, unless otherwise specified, shall be paid by:

(a) Cash, but not over $_____ ;

(b) Good certified check of Purchaser drawn on or official check issued by any bank, savings bank, trust company or savings and loan association having a banking office in the State of New York, unendorsed and payable to the order of Seller, or as Seller may otherwise direct upon reasonable prior notice (by telephone or otherwise) to Purchaser;

(c) As to money other than the purchase price payable to Seller at Closing, uncertified check of Purchaser up to the amount of $_____ ; and

(d) As otherwise agreed to in writing by Seller or Seller's attorney.

8. Mortgage Commitment Contingency.

(a) The obligation of Purchaser to purchase under this contract is conditioned upon issuance, on or before _____ days after a fully executed copy of this contract is given to Purchaser or Purchaser's attorney in the manner set forth in paragraph 25 or subparagraph 8(k) (the "Commitment Date"), of a written commitment from an Institutional Lender pursuant to which such Institutional Lender agrees to make a first mortgage loan, other than a VA, FHA, or other governmentally insured loan, to Purchaser, at Purchaser's sole cost and expense, of $_____ for a term of at least _____ years (or such lesser sum or shorter term as Purchaser shall be willing to accept) at the prevailing fixed or adjustable rate of interest and on other customary commitment terms (the **"Commitment"**). To the extent a Commitment is conditioned on the sale of Purchaser's current home, payment of any outstanding debt, no material adverse change in Purchaser's financial condition or any other customary conditions,

Purchaser accepts the risk that such conditions may not be met; however, a commitment conditioned on the Institutional Lender's approval of an appraisal shall not be deemed a "Commitment" hereunder until an appraisal is approved (and if that does not occur before the Commitment Date, Purchaser may cancel under subparagraph 8(e) unless the Commitment Date is extended). Purchaser's obligations hereunder are conditioned only on issuance of a Commitment. Once a Commitment is issued, Purchaser is bound under this contract even if the lender fails or refuses to fund the loan for any reason.

(b) Purchaser shall (i) make prompt application to one or, at Purchaser's election, more than one Institutional Lender for such mortgage loan, (ii) furnish accurate and complete information regarding Purchaser and members of Purchaser's family, as required, (iii) pay all fees, points and charges required in connection with such application and loan, (iv) pursue such application with diligence, and (v) cooperate in good faith with such Institutional Lender(s) to obtain a Commitment. Purchaser shall accept a Commitment meeting the terms set forth in subparagraph 8(a) and shall comply with all requirements of such Commitment (or any other commitment accepted by Purchaser). Purchaser shall furnish Seller with a copy of the Commitment promptly after receipt thereof.

(c) [*Delete this subparagraph if inapplicable*] Prompt submission by Purchaser of an application to a mortgage broker registered pursuant to Article 12 D of the New York Banking Law (**"Mortgage Broker"**) shall constitute full compliance with the terms and conditions set forth in subparagraph 8(b)(i), provided that such Mortgage Broker promptly submits such application to such Institutional Lender(s). Purchaser shall cooperate in good faith with such Mortgage Broker to obtain a Commitment from such Institutional Lender(s).

(d) If all Institutional Lenders to whom applications were made deny such applications in writing prior to the Commitment Date, Purchaser may cancel this contract by giving Notice thereof to Seller, with a copy of such denials, provided that Purchaser has complied with all its obligations under this paragraph 8.

(e) If no Commitment is issued by the Institutional Lender on or before the Commitment Date, then, unless Purchaser has accepted a written commitment from an Institutional Lender that does not conform to the terms set forth in subparagraph 8(a), Purchaser may cancel this contract by giving Notice to Seller within 5 business days after the Commitment Date, provided that such Notice includes the name and address of the Institutional Lender(s) to whom application was made and that Purchaser has complied with all its obligations under this paragraph 8.

(f) If this contract is canceled by Purchaser pursuant to subparagraphs 8(d) or (e), neither party shall thereafter have any further rights against, or obligations or liabilities to, the other by reason of this contract, except that the Downpayment shall be promptly refunded to Purchaser and except as set forth in paragraph 27.

(g) If Purchaser fails to give timely Notice of cancellation or if Purchaser accepts a written commitment from an Institutional Lender that does not conform to the terms set forth in subparagraph 8(a), then Purchaser shall be deemed to have waived Purchaser's right to cancel this contract and to receive a refund of the Downpayment by reason of the contingency contained in this paragraph 8.

(h) If Seller has not received a copy of a commitment from an Institutional Lender accepted by Purchaser by the Commitment Date, Seller may cancel this contract by giving Notice to Purchaser within 5 business days after the Commitment Date, which cancellation shall become effective unless Purchaser delivers a copy of such commitment to Seller within 10 business days after the Commitment Date. After such cancellation neither party shall have any further rights against, or obligations or liabilities to, the other by reason of this contract, except that the Downpayment shall be promptly refunded to Purchaser (provided Purchaser has complied with all of its obligations under this paragraph 8) and except as set forth in paragraph 27.

(i) The attorneys for the parties are hereby authorized to give and receive on behalf of their clients all Notices and deliveries under this paragraph 8.

(j) For purposes of this contract, the term "Institutional Lender" shall mean any bank, savings bank, private banker, trust company, savings and loan association, credit union or similar banking institution whether organized under the laws of this state, the United States or any other state; foreign banking corporation licensed by the Superintendent of Banks of New York or regulated by the Comptroller of the Currency to transact business in New York State; insurance company duly organized or licensed to do business in New York State; mortgage banker licensed pursuant to Article 12-D of the Banking Law; and any instrumentality created by the United States or any state with the power to make mortgage loans.

(k) For purposes of subparagraph (a), Purchaser shall be deemed to have been given a fully executed copy of this contract on the _____ business day following the date of ordinary or regular mailing, postage prepaid.

9. Permitted Exceptions. The Premises are sold and shall be conveyed subject to:

(a) Zoning and subdivision laws and regulations, and landmark, historic or wetlands designation, provided that they are not violated by the existing buildings and improvements erected on the property or their use;

(b) Consents for the erection of any structures on, under or above any streets on which the Premises abut;

(c) Encroachments of stoops, areas, cellar steps, trim and cornices, if any, upon any street or highway;

(d) Real estate taxes that are a lien, but are not yet due and payable; and

(e) The other matters, if any, including a survey exception, set forth in a Rider attached.

10. Governmental Violations and Orders.

(a) Seller shall comply with all notes or notices of violations of law or municipal ordinances, orders or requirements noted or issued as of the date hereof by any governmental department having authority as to lands, housing, buildings, fire, health, environmental and labor conditions affecting the Premises. The Premises shall be conveyed free of them at Closing. Seller shall furnish Purchaser with any authorizations necessary to make the searches that could disclose these matters.

(b) [*Delete if inapplicable*] All obligations affecting the Premises pursuant to the Administrative Code of the City of New York incurred prior to Closing and payable in money shall be discharged by Seller at or prior to Closing.

11. Seller's Representations.

(a) Seller represents and warrants to Purchaser that:

(i) The Premises abut or have a right of access to a public road;

(ii) Seller is the sole owner of the Premises and has the full right, power and authority to sell, convey and transfer the same in accordance with the terms of this contract;

(iii) Seller is not a "foreign person," as that term is defined for purposes of the Foreign Investment in Real Property Tax Act, Internal Revenue Code (**"IRC"**) Section 1445, as amended, and the regulations promulgated thereunder (collectively **"FIRPTA"**);

(iv) The Premises are not affected by any exemptions or abatements of taxes; and

(v) Seller has been known by no other name for the past ten years, except

_____.

(b) Seller covenants and warrants that all of the representations and warranties set forth in this contract shall be true and correct at Closing.

(c) Except as otherwise expressly set forth in this contract, none of Seller's covenants, representations, warranties or other obligations contained in this contract shall survive Closing.

12. Condition of Property.

Purchaser acknowledges and represents that Purchaser is fully aware of the physical condition and state of repair of the Premises and of all other property included in this sale, based on Purchaser's own inspection and investigation thereof, and that Purchaser is entering into this contract based solely upon such inspection and investigation and not upon any information, data, statements or representations, written or oral, as to the physical condition, state of repair, use, cost of operation or any other matter related to the Premises or the other property included in the sale, given or made by Seller or its representatives, and shall accept the same "as is" in their present condition and state of repair, subject to reasonable use, wear, tear and natural deterioration between the date hereof and the date of Closing, except as otherwise set forth in paragraph 16(e), without any reduction in the purchase price or claim of any kind for any change in such condition by reason thereof subsequent to the date of this contract. Purchaser and its authorized representatives shall have the right, at reasonable times and upon reasonable notice (by telephone or otherwise) to Seller, to inspect the Premises before Closing.

13. Insurable Title.

Seller shall give and Purchaser shall accept such title as _____ shall be willing to approve and insure in accordance with its standard form of title policy approved by the New York State Insurance Department, subject only to the matters provided for in this contract.

14. Closing, Deed and Title.

(a) **"Closing"** means the settlement of the obligations of Seller and Purchaser to each other under this contract, including the payment of the purchase price to Seller, and the delivery to Purchaser of a deed in proper statutory short form for record, duly executed and acknowledged, so as to convey to Purchaser fee simple title to the Premises, free of all encumbrances, except as otherwise herein stated. The deed shall contain a covenant by Seller as required by subd. 5 of Section 13 of the Lien Law.

(b) If Seller is a corporation, it shall deliver to Purchaser at the time of Closing (i) a resolution of its Board of Directors authorizing the sale and delivery of the deed, and (ii) a certificate by the Secretary or Assistant Secretary of the corporation certifying such resolution and setting forth facts showing that the transfer is in conformity with the requirements of Section 909 of the Business Corporation Law. The deed in such case shall contain a recital sufficient to establish compliance with that Section.

15. Closing Date and Place.

Closing shall take place at the office of _____ at _____ o'clock on _____ or, upon reasonable notice (by telephone or otherwise) by Purchaser, at the office of _____.

16. Conditions to Closing.

This contract and Purchaser's obligation to purchase the Premises are also subject to and conditioned upon the fulfillment of the following conditions precedent:

(a) The accuracy, as of the date of Closing, of the representations and warranties of Seller made in this contract.

(b) The delivery by Seller to Purchaser of a valid and subsisting Certificate of Occupancy or other required certificate of compliance, or evidence that none was required, covering the building(s) and all of the other improvements located on the property authorizing their use as a _____ at the date of Closing.

(c) The delivery by Seller to Purchaser of a certificate stating that Seller is not a foreign person, which certificate shall be in the form then required by FIRPTA or a withholding certificate from the Internal Revenue Service. If Seller fails to deliver the aforesaid certificate or if Purchaser is not entitled under FIRPTA to rely on such certificate, Purchaser shall deduct and withhold from the purchase price a sum equal to 10% thereof (or any lesser amount permitted by law) and shall at Closing remit the withheld amount with the required forms to the Internal Revenue Service.

(d) The delivery of the Premises and all building(s) and improvements comprising a part thereof in broom clean condition, vacant and free of leases or tenancies, together with keys to the Premises.

(e) All plumbing (including water supply and septic systems, if any), heating and air conditioning, if any, electrical and mechanical systems, equipment and machinery in the building(s) located on the property and all appliances which are included in this sale being in working order as of the date of Closing.

(f) If the Premises are a one or two family house, delivery by the parties at Closing of affidavits in compliance with state and local law requirements to the effect that there is installed in the Premises a smoke detecting alarm device or devices.

(g) The delivery by the parties of any other affidavits required as a condition of recording the deed.

17. Deed Transfer and Recording Taxes.

At Closing, certified or official bank checks payable to the order of the appropriate State, City or County officer in the amount of any applicable transfer and/or recording tax payable by reason of the delivery or recording of the deed or mortgage, if any, shall be delivered by the party required by law or by this contract to pay such transfer and/or recording tax, together with any required tax returns duly executed and sworn to, and such party shall cause any such checks and returns to be delivered to the appropriate officer promptly after Closing. The obligation to pay any additional tax or deficiency and any interest or penalties thereon shall survive Closing.

18. Apportionments and Other Adjustments; Water Meter and Installment Assessments.

(a) To the extent applicable, the following shall be apportioned as of midnight of the day before the day of Closing: (i) taxes, water charges and sewer rents, on the basis of the fiscal period for which assessed; (ii) fuel; (iii) interest on the existing mortgage; (iv) premiums on existing transferable insurance policies and renewals of those expiring prior to Closing; (v) vault charges; (vi) rents as and when collected.

(b) If Closing shall occur before a new tax rate is fixed, the apportionment of taxes shall be upon the basis of the tax rate for the immediately preceding fiscal period applied to the latest assessed valuation.

(c) If there is a water meter on the Premises, Seller shall furnish a reading to a date not more than 30 days before Closing and the unfixed meter charge and sewer rent, if any, shall be apportioned on the basis of such last reading.

(d) If at the date of Closing the Premises are affected by an assessment which is or may become payable in annual installments, and the first installment is then a lien, or has been paid, then for the purposes of this contract all the unpaid installments shall be considered due and shall be paid by Seller at or prior to Closing.

(e) Any errors or omissions in computing apportionments or other adjustments at Closing shall be corrected within a reasonable time following Closing. This subparagraph shall survive Closing.

19. Allowance for Unpaid Taxes, etc.

Seller has the option to credit Purchaser as an adjustment to the purchase price with the amount of any unpaid taxes, assessments, water charges and sewer rents, together with any interest and penalties thereon to a date not less than five business days after Closing, provided that official bills therefor computed to said date are produced at Closing.

20. Use of Purchase Price to Remove Encumbrances.

If at Closing there are other liens or encumbrances that Seller is obligated to pay or discharge, Seller may use any portion of the cash balance of the purchase price to pay or discharge them, provided Seller shall simultaneously deliver to Purchaser at Closing instruments in recordable form and sufficient to satisfy such liens or encumbrances of record, together with the cost of recording or filing said instruments. As an alternative Seller may deposit sufficient monies with the title insurance company employed by Purchaser acceptable to and required by it to assure their discharge, but only if the title insurance company will insure Purchaser's title clear of the matters or insure against their enforcement out of the Premises and will insure Purchaser's Institutional Lender clear of such matters. Upon reasonable prior notice (by telephone or otherwise), Purchaser shall provide separate certified or official bank checks as requested to assist in clearing up these matters.

21. Title Examination; Seller's Inability to Convey; Limitations of Liability.

(a) Purchaser shall order an examination of title in respect of the Premises from a title company licensed or authorized to issue title insurance by the New York

State Insurance Department or any agent for such title company promptly after the execution of this contract or, if this contract is subject to the mortgage contingency set forth in paragraph 8, after a mortgage commitment has been accepted by Purchaser. Purchaser shall cause a copy of the title report and of any additions thereto to be delivered to the attorney(s) for Seller promptly after receipt thereof.

(b) (i) If at the date of Closing Seller is unable to transfer title to Purchaser in accordance with this contract, or Purchaser has other valid grounds for refusing to close, whether by reason of liens, encumbrances or other objections to title or otherwise (herein collectively called **"Defects"**), other than those subject to which Purchaser is obligated to accept title hereunder or which Purchaser may have waived and other than those which Seller has herein expressly agreed to remove, remedy or discharge and if Purchaser shall be unwilling to waive the same and to close title without abatement of the purchase price, then, except as hereinafter set forth, Seller shall have the right, at Seller's sole election, either to take such action as Seller may deem advisable to remove, remedy, discharge or comply with such Defects or to cancel this contract; (ii) if Seller elects to take action to remove, remedy or comply with such Defects, Seller shall be entitled from time to time, upon Notice to Purchaser, to adjourn the date for Closing hereunder for a period or periods not exceeding _____ days in the aggregate (but not extending beyond the date upon which Purchaser's mortgage commitment, if any, shall expire), and the date for Closing shall be adjourned to a date specified by Seller not beyond such period. If for any reason whatsoever, Seller shall not have succeeded in removing, remedying or complying with such Defects at the expiration of such adjournment(s), and if Purchaser shall still be unwilling to waive the same and to close title without abatement of the purchase price, then either party may cancel this contract by Notice to the other given within 10 days after such adjourned date; (iii) notwithstanding the foregoing, the existing mortgage (unless this sale is subject to the same) and any matter created by Seller after the date hereof shall be released, discharged or otherwise cured by Seller at or prior to Closing.

(c) If this contract is cancelled pursuant to its terms, other than as a result of Purchaser's default, this contract shall terminate and come to an end, and neither party shall have any further rights, obligations or liabilities against or to the other hereunder or otherwise, except that: (i) Seller shall promptly refund or cause the Escrowee to refund the Downpayment to Purchaser and, unless cancelled as a result of Purchaser's default or pursuant to paragraph 8, to reimburse Purchaser for the net cost of examination of title, including any appropriate additional charges related thereto, and the net cost, if actually paid or incurred by Purchaser, for updating the existing survey of the Premises or of a new survey, and (ii) the obligations under paragraph 27 shall survive the termination of this contract.

22. Affidavit as to Judgments, Bankruptcies, etc.

If a title examination discloses judgments, bankruptcies or other returns against persons having names the same as or similar to that of Seller, Seller shall deliver an affidavit at Closing showing that they are not against Seller.

23. Defaults and Remedies.

(a) If Purchaser defaults hereunder, Seller's sole remedy shall be to receive and retain the Downpayment as liquidated damages, it being agreed that Seller's damages in case of Purchaser's default might be impossible to ascertain and that the Downpayment constitutes a fair and reasonable amount of damages under the circumstances and is not a penalty.

(b) If Seller defaults hereunder, Purchaser shall have such remedies as Purchaser shall be entitled to at law or in equity, including, but not limited to, specific performance.

24. Purchaser's Lien.

All money paid on account of this contract, and the reasonable expenses of examination of title to the Premises and of any survey and survey inspection charges, are hereby made liens on the Premises, but such liens shall not continue after default by Purchaser under this contract.

25. Notices.

Any notice or other communication (**"Notice"**) shall be in writing and either:

(a) sent by either of the parties hereto or by their respective attorneys who are hereby authorized to do so on their behalf or by the Escrowee, by registered or certified mail, postage prepaid, or

(b) delivered in person or by overnight courier, with receipt acknowledged, to the respective addresses given in this contract for the party and the Escrowee, to whom the Notice is to be given, or to such other address as such party or Escrowee shall hereafter designate by Notice given to the other party or parties and the Escrowee pursuant to this paragraph. Each Notice mailed shall be deemed given on the third business day following the date of mailing the same, except that any notice to Escrowee shall be deemed given only upon receipt by Escrowee and each Notice delivered in person or by overnight courier shall be deemed given when delivered, or

(c) with respect to paragraph 7(b) or 20, sent by fax to the party's attorney. Each notice by fax shall be deemed given when transmission is confirmed by the sender's fax machine. A copy of each notice sent to a party shall also be sent to the party's attorney. The attorneys for the parties are hereby authorized to give and receive on behalf of their clients all Notices and deliveries.

26. No Assignment.

This contract may not be assigned by Purchaser without the prior written consent of Seller in each instance and any purported assignment(s) made without such consent shall be void.

27. Broker.

Seller and Purchaser each represents and warrants to the other that it has not dealt with any real estate broker in connection with this sale other than _____ (**"Broker"**) and Seller shall pay Broker any commission earned pursuant to a separate agreement between Seller and Broker. Seller and Purchaser shall indemnify and defend each other against any costs, claims and expenses, including reasonable attorneys' fees, arising out of the breach on their respective parts of any representation or agreement contained in this paragraph. The provisions of this paragraph shall survive Closing or, if Closing does not occur, the termination of this contract.

28. Miscellaneous.

(a) All prior understandings, agreements, representations and warranties, oral or written, between Seller and Purchaser are merged in this contract; it completely expresses their full agreement and has been entered into after full investigation, neither party relying upon any statement made by anyone else that is not set forth in this contract.

(b) Neither this contract nor any provision thereof may be waived, changed or cancelled except in writing. This contract shall also apply to and bind the heirs, distributes, legal representatives, successors and permitted assigns of the respective parties. The parties hereby authorize their respective attorneys to agree in writing to any changes in dates and time periods provided for in this contract.

(c) Any singular word or term herein shall also be read as in the plural and the neuter shall include the masculine and feminine gender, whenever the sense of this contract may require it.

(d) The captions in this contract are for convenience of reference only and in no way define, limit or describe the scope of this contract and shall not be considered in the interpretation of this contract or any provision hereof.

(e) This contract shall not be binding or effective until duly executed and delivered by Seller and Purchaser.

(f) Seller and Purchaser shall comply with IRC reporting requirements, if applicable. This subparagraph shall survive Closing.

(g) Each party shall, at any time and from time to time, execute, acknowledge where appropriate and deliver such further instruments and documents and take such other action as may be reasonably requested by the other in order to carry out the intent and purpose of this contract. This subparagraph shall survive Closing.

(h) This contract is intended for the exclusive benefit of the parties hereto and, except as otherwise expressly provided herein, shall not be for the benefit of, and shall not create any rights in, or be enforceable by, any other person or entity.

(i) If applicable, the complete and fully executed disclosure of information on lead based paint and/or lead based paint hazards is attached hereto and made a part hereof.

IN WITNESS WHEREOF, this contract has been duly executed by the parties hereto.

Seller:	Purchaser:
_____	_____
_____	_____
Attorney for Seller:	Attorney for Purchaser:
_____	_____
Name	Name
_____	_____
Address:	Address:
_____	_____
Tel.:	Tel.:
_____	_____
Fax:	Fax:
_____	_____

Receipt of the Downpayment is acknowledged and the undersigned agrees to act in accordance with the provisions of paragraph 6 above.

Escrowee

PREMISES:

Section: _____

Block: _____

Lot: _____

County or Town: _____

Street No. Address: _____

Resources

Commercial property search websites:

commercialsearch.realtor.com, www.cbcworldwide.com, www.costar.com, www.loopnet.com, www.trulia.com

Definitions and financial terms:

www.investopedia.com

Information on landlord and tenant rights and responsibilities:

www.nolo.com

Mortgage calculators and interest rate data:

www.bankrate.com

Tool for analyzing regions:

www.bls.gov, www.census.gov, www.city-data.com, www.loopnet.com

Glossary

bond: A debt investment in which the investor agrees to loan money to a corporation or government entity in exchange for a predetermined interest rate. Bonds are generally classified as fixed-income securities.

capital gain: The increase in value of an asset, such as real estate or a financial security like a stock or a bond. Investors usually face a tax liability on the increase in value relative to the asset's purchase prices, but in most cases they need not pay taxes on such gains until they sell the asset. When property declines in value below its purchase price, an investor incurs a **capital loss.**

capitalization rate (cap rate): Net operating income divided by the value of a property.

carrying costs: The costs of holding an asset. When you buy corn, you must pay to store it. When you buy real estate, you must pay taxes and maintenance costs. Real property and physical commodities tend to incur higher carrying costs than financial investments.

cash flow: A stream of revenue. In a real estate context, most cash flows come from rents and leases. If expenses exceed revenue, cash flows will turn negative, possibly forcing the property owner to chip in personal funds to cover costs.

cash-on-cash return: A property's cash flows divided by the amount of cash an investor put up to buy that property. This is the closest the typical real estate investor will get to a bottom line.

collateral: Assets a borrower pledges to a lender as security for a loan. In other words, if you borrow against the value of your property, you have, in effect, pledged it as collateral. If you stop paying on the loan, the lender may confiscate the collateral and sell it to repay the debt.

corporation: A legal entity distinct from its owners. Corporations can borrow money, enforce contracts, and do many things an individual can do. However, business owners who incorporate can limit their personal liability for damage caused by the corporation's actions.

covenant: A promise connected to a loan designed to protect a lender against default. Common covenants include the borrower pledging to provide additional information, meet specific financial goals, or avoid borrowing additional money. When borrowers violate a covenant, the loan may come due immediately.

deduction: A cost subtracted from taxable income. Expenses that qualify as deductible allow an investor to reduce tax liability.

depreciation: An accounting tool that allocates the cost of an asset over time. Businesses depreciate for both accounting and tax purposes, and they can choose from several methods.

diversification: The use of multiple investments to protect against weakness in some portions of the market. People who own a diverse basket of investments can theoretically earn higher returns with lower risk than most of the investments would on their own. Real estate is a powerful diversification tool relative to more widely held investments, such as stocks and bonds.

due diligence: The level of care a reasonable person takes before making a financial transaction. In the real estate context, it refers to reviewing financial records, inspecting the property, and any other actions needed to ensure the buyer won't receive any surprises after closing.

equity: The value of a piece of property minus the amount still owed on it. If the property owner sold the real estate and used the proceeds to pay off the mortgage, the cash remaining after the payoff would be the property's equity.

hedge: An investment designed to reduce the risk of poor returns for a particular asset. For example, an investor who owns a stock index might protect against declines in that index by purchasing a futures contract that rises in value when the index falls. Because real estate tends to increase in value during periods of high inflation, it serves as a partial hedge against declines in other investments that react poorly to rising consumer prices.

interest: The charge borrowers pay for the privilege of using someone else's money.

leverage: The use of borrowed money to finance the purchase of property. Debt allows investors to acquire real estate worth far more than their cash on hand. However, payments on that debt raise the risk that the property's cash flows won't cover all the expenses. An investor who has borrowed a lot of money relative to the value of the property is said to be highly leveraged.

limited liability company (LLC): A type of corporation that insulates members from liability for the company's debts.

loan-to-value ratio: The amount borrowed relative to the worth of the property. If a bank allows an investor to borrow at a loan-to-value ratio of 75 percent, he can acquire a $1 million office building by putting up $250,000 in cash (25 percent of the value) while the bank provides the remaining $750,000 (75 percent of the value).

mortgage: A loan secured by real estate. Borrowers must pay the loan back in regularly scheduled installments, generally over a number of years. Because of the long terms of mortgage loans, in the early years, most of a borrower's payments will go toward interest, with little paying down the loan's principal.

net operating income: Potential rental income minus operating expenses.

principal: The amount of a loan still owed, not counting interest. For example, suppose an investor borrowed $100,000 over 15 years and then repaid $25,000 during the first year of the loan, with $7,000 of that money going to interest costs. That leaves $18,000 to put toward reducing the amount owed, bringing the principal down to $82,000.

property manager: A person or company overseeing the day-to-day operations of a piece of real estate.

real estate: Land and permanent structures erected on it.

real estate investment trust (REIT): A company that invests directly in real estate and sells ownership interests through exchanges like a stock. REITs can own either real property or mortgage loans. These companies enjoy special tax treatment that allows them to return higher cash flows to investors than most stocks can offer. Through REITs, investors can purchase a stake in the real estate market without the liquidity risk (you can sell REITs in real time just like stocks) or the hassles of managing property.

renovation reserves: Cash a property owner sets aside to use for repairs and upgrades to the building.

return: The gain or loss of an investment in a given period. Returns include both income and capital gains, or price appreciation.

risk-adjusted return: A measurement of an investment's return relative to the amount of risk needed to produce that return.

risk tolerance: The amount of volatility an investor can take. Willingness and ability to absorb investment fluctuations varies greatly from person to person. Investors of any tolerance can make money, but they can improve their odds by not taking on more risk than they can handle. Too much risk can spark fear, which in turn leads to poor investment decisions.

standard deviation: A measurement of how widely returns are dispersed around the average. The broader the variation, the higher the standard deviation, and thus the greater an investment's volatility, or risk.

stock: An ownership interest in a company. Over long periods, stocks tend to provide higher returns than bonds or real estate, but at the cost of greater volatility.

yield: The ratio of dividends or other cash payouts to the price of a security. For example, if a REIT trades at $50 per share and pays an annual dividend of $2.50 per share, it yields 5 percent (2.50/50).

Bibliography

"2013 Lodging Industry Profile." American Hotel & Lodging Association. Accessed January 2014. www.ahla.com/content.aspx?id=35603.

Chavis, Brian. *Buy It, Rent It, Profit!* New York: Fireside, 2009.

"Commercial Real Estate." Merrill Lynch Wealth Management, June 2012. www.wealthmanagement.ml.com/publish/content/application/pdf/GWMOL /Commercial-Real-Estate-2012.pdf?campaign=TRQA1.

"Donald Trump." *Forbes* profile page, September 2013. www.forbes.com/profile /donald-trump.

"Emerging Trends in Real Estate 2013." Urban Land Institute and PwC, October 2012. www.uli.org/wp-content/uploads/ULI-Documents/Emerging-Trends-in -Real-Estate-US-2013.pdf.

"Financial Accounts of the United States." Federal Reserve, December 9, 2013. www.federalreserve.gov/releases/z1.

"Historical Census of Housing Tables." U.S. Census Bureau, October 31, 2011. www.census.gov/hhes/www/housing/census/historic/grossrents.html.

"Housing Data." National Association of Home Builders. Accessed January 2014. www.nahb.org/page.aspx/landing/sectionID=113.

2013 Ibbotson SBBI Classic Yearbook. Chicago: Morningstar, 2013, p. 38.

Landlord/tenant liability issues. Nolo.com. Accessed January 2014. www.nolo.com.

"NCREIF Property Index Returns." National Council of Real Estate Investment Fiduciaries. Accessed December 2013. www.ncreif.org/property-index -returns.aspx.

"Real Estate Appreciation." Advantage Software. Accessed December 2013. www.invest-2win.com/appreciation.html.

Real estate prices from LoopNet.com. Accessed January 2014. www.loopnet.com.

"Research & Statistics," National Association of Realtors. Accessed January 2014. www.realtor.org/research-and-statistics.

"Residential Vacancies and Homeownership." U.S. Census Bureau, November 5, 2013. www.census.gov/housing/hvs/files/qtr313/q313press.pdf.

"Tips & Advice." *Redfin* (blog). Accessed January 2014. blog.redfin.com/blog/2008 /05/15_questions_to_ask_when_hiring_a_real_estate_agent.html#.UsSvh_RDuSo.

"Top Ten Frivolous Lawsuits." LegalZoom, October 2007. www.legalzoom.com /lawsuits-settlements/personal-injury/top-ten-frivolous-lawsuits.

Various definitions and financial terms. Investopedia.com. Accessed January 2014. www.investopedia.com.

"What Does Donald Trump Really Own?" *The Real Deal,* July 1, 2013. www.therealdeal.com/issues_articles/the-8-billion-dollar-man.

"What to Expect When Applying for a Commercial Mortgage Loan." http://RealEstateABC.com. Accessed January 2014. www.realestateabc.com /loanguide/applying-commercial1.htm.

"Why You Should Be Investing Your Money in Real Estate." *Entrepreneur,* September 23, 2013. www.entrepreneur.com/article/228506.

Index